JOAN OCEAN

Dolphin Connection

INTERDIMENSIONAL WAYS OF LIVING

Art by Jean-Luc Bozzoli

A Dolphin Connection Book

Hawaii

1989

DOLPHIN CONNECTION: INTERDIMENSIONAL WAYS OF LIVING

A Dolphin Connection Book

Second Printing, 1996

Cover Art, Book Design, Illustrations and Photography: Jean-Luc Bozzoli ©

First Printing:
Production & Computer Consultant: Ken Kimura
Computer Color Separations: Joel Lovingfoss
Linotronic Typesetting: Belknap Productions, Honolulu, Hawaii
Editing: Shirley Reaume, Kym L. Miller, William Spencer, and Joe Garofalow
Printed by Globe Press Pty Ltd in Melbourne

Second Printing:
Production & Computer Consultant: Suchi Psarakos
Cover Color Separations: Belknap Imaging, Honolulu, Hawaii

Library of Congress Catalog Card Number: 89-81370

Ocean, Joan
        Dolphin Connection: Interdimensional Ways of Living
        Includes bibliographical references and glossary.
        1. Ocean, Joan   2. Metaphysics.   3. Human-animal relationships.
        4. Dolphins.   5. Whales.   I. Dolphin Connection. II. Title.

ISBN: 0 949679 10 0

Published in the United States by
Dolphin Connection
P.O. Box 275
Kailua, Hawaii, USA 96734

This book is dedicated

with Deep Gratitude and Love

to the Wonder and Beauty of our giving planet

and its Creative Source

ACKNOWLEDGEMENT

This book is written for all of you who wrote to me
and shared your hopes and dreams.

This is your story too.

Your compassion and commitment
are an inspiration to me.

May all the love in your heart
be returned to you ten-fold.

THANK YOU

IN GRATITUDE

My greatest inspiration comes from the thousands of people who responded so enthusiastically and lovingly to the Dolphin Connection audio-visual presentations. Your radiant smiles and heartwarming letters have led to my decision to put into words a dolphin communication process that is beyond words.

I gratefully acknowledge the following people for their friendship and inspiration: Jean-Luc Bozzoli; Cyril and Agnes Phillips, my parents; Lisa, Laura and Frank Joseph Garofalow, my children; Dr. John Lilly, Dr. Frank Alper, Stephen Bellamy, Itzak Bentov, Genevieve and Serge Bozzoli, Dr. Jerry Corey, Gigi Coyle, Evelyn Durkas, Diana Fairechild, Frank Garofalow, Patricia Hooper, Kamala Hope-Campbell, Duane Judge, Ken Kimura, Roxanne Kremer, Tysen Mueller, Katie and Jim Nollman, Lorraine O'Grady, Charles Phillips, Suchi Psarakos, Dr. Carl Rogers, Linda Tellington-Jones, and Dhyani Ywahoo.

I also acknowledge all the dolphins, swimming freely and in captivity, who willingly became my friends and teachers. I support and encourage interactions by invitation with dolphins who live in the ocean. I also understand the transformative impact of my own contacts with domesticated dolphins. For those early experiences, I express my deep love to the guru dolphins (GURU — Gee, U are U !) who offer themselves to humanity's search for happiness, and who unconditionally nudged me along !

Their love for the ocean, the Earth, and their own family pods was communicated to me, and I remembered my own cellular connections to the same.

Through their playfulness, they have encouraged me to remain with my dreams for a Transformational Theater and Community.

And the wonderful part of all this is.......

WE HAVE JUST <u>BEGUN</u> TO PLAY TOGETHER !!!

Joan Ocean
Hawaii, 1989

TABLE OF CONTENTS

INTRODUCTION

My life was changed by contacts with dolphins and whales. This book is a personal account of my experiences, and a story of praise for the pods of dolphins that I encountered. I have no reservations about calling them my friends, and even teachers. They have been teachers in the truest sense of the word... they are living examples of a way of life that expresses joy, harmony and health.

In addition, I am fascinated by the study of dolphins in relation to my twenty-two years background as a psychologist. For many years I have counselled the families of abused children, finding safe homes for the children when their lives were endangered and representing them in the courts. Over another period of many years, I counselled and played athletic activities with mentally disturbed adults who were labeled as manic-depressives, brain damaged and schizophrenic. I assisted women who were in the operating room of an abortion clinic for incest victims and counselled alcohol and drug addicts. Often I felt discouraged in this work. Clients making breakthroughs in setting affirmative life goals, regressed eventually to the old problematic attitudes and self-denying behaviors. Deeply caring about these people, I spent many evenings in prayer and contemplation, asking for better ways to help and inspire them.

When I experienced the profound and enriching changes occurring in my life after swims with dolphins, I felt strongly that these experiences would be life enhancing for anyone who chose to interact with dolphins in this way.

My personal philosophy of change and growth reflected a process of joy, not pain. And prescribed my clients' choices be freely made, assisted by short-term counselling, with an outcome leading to an expansive lifestyle. Suffering and long-term lamenting were the antithesis of a healthy life, and not to be encouraged.

Swimming with dolphins is always a pleasant experience that leads to extensive soul-searching, filled with the excitement of many wonderful possibilities. Every new decision is an outgrowth of optimism and joy. More than that, the feelings and choices do not dissipate with time, but instead lead to more freedom in our life and work. If ever I begin to doubt my ability to fulfill my plans, another dip with the dolphins returns me to a positive perspective.

In 1978, after meeting John C. Lilly, M.D., world pioneer in human-dolphin communications, I began to dream about dolphins. When I started receiving messages from dolphins in 1984, I told very few people. Then in 1985 a friend published one of my dolphin messages in a newsletter. The response from people who felt they had had similar communications was immediate and so supportive that I began to publish dolphin messages on notecards and in articles. Today, many people are revealing their empathic communications with dolphins.

In my contacts with dolphin trainers, ecologists, marine researchers and others who interact with cetaceans, I learned that every one of them has experienced a telepathic communication between themselves and the dolphins or whales. However, for career or personal reasons, they prefer not to focus on those types of interactions. It is uncertain and unsettling for them. It is an unknown.

I am not a 'scientist' nor an 'experimental psychologist,' but I am interested in exploring this telepathic exchange with cetaceans as a way to help people understand themselves, their relationship to Nature and the universe in which we live.

Changing our lifestyle became a paramount concern for many in the 1980s. It appears that the human race is about to become obsolete. Along with "Save the Whales" and "Save the Trees", the slogan aptly put is, "Save the People !"

There is an upsurge of a new breed of people who silently care for the Earth in small, personal ways, and whose expertise is needed now to educate the greater population on how to do likewise.

Where else can people turn for suggestions and help?

The turn to the sea was foreseeable. Large-brained dolphins and whales have lived peaceably in their environment for fifty million years without destroying the Earth. There is much we can learn from them.

The communication with cetaceans gains urgency as humanity realizes science and technology do not have solutions for averting disaster. The lucrative attraction for inappropriate technology has led to a life estranged from Nature, sanctioning the demise of our life-support systems.

But do not despair. It is all part of a larger plan that takes us to the height of our folly as a way of stimulating change, and prepares us for entry into advanced systems of communication and living.

Dolphins have information that contains solutions for us. Their means of teaching will not mirror our old paradigms of intellectual hypothesis building in the name of 'science.' Their communication-of-information challenges us to expand our intelligence capabilities and use new receptors in our body. It is in itself a solution to many problems since it increases our perceptions of the natural world. Dolphins are not merely sending us information, they are showing us an entirely new method of understanding, experiencing and interacting with our environment.

In my own process of illumination, I understand the transforming power of compassion and empathy. I feel the dolphins communicate TELEMPATHICALLY. As a psychologist, empathy is a significant part of my ability to help others. EMPATHY. A particularly interesting word. It contains within it the words MY PATH and THE MAP. Had I noticed this earlier in my dolphin work, I would have quickly understood my experiences of communication with the dolphins. (Thank you, Linda Goodman ! Appendix)

This book is about my learning to experience the cetaceans' aesthetic holograms of communication, and about the joy that accompanies this expanded awareness.

1

THE AWAKENING

You are the voice of many for the millennium....

The Nine of Sirius B

This is the time of becoming. Our spiritual paths often lead us into unknown places, stretching our beliefs and our wisdom. We are wearing many hats. From one moment to the next we are healers, awakeners, meditators and activists, scientists, seers, students, teachers, speakers, listeners, global citizens and galactic ambassadors. All of those things, plus many more, in each of us.

This was hardly understandable to me, as I sat with a group of people at Esalen Institute in Big Sur, California, 1978, participating in a workshop about personal growth and peak experiences. The workshop facilitator explained she had become a trans-channeler while in England where she assisted the police in locating missing persons. She would now demonstrate her skills to any of us in the group who would like to ask questions of the off-planet entities who assisted her. I was curious, but doubtful. I had no questions to ask.

As other participants began to ask about their physical health and their careers, I was surprised to notice the answers to their questions were filling my own mind at the same time the channeler was speedily recording the answers in automatic writing on paper. The sensitive information was so detailed, transparent, and loving that I began to listen to this psychic exchange with interest.

The incoming energy field identified itself as "The Nine" saying they had the radiation of any number from one to nine and they were of the vibrational intensity of the light of Sirius B, a star system that is 8.6 light years from our sun. (Glossary)

As I continued to interact with the energies of The Nine during this one-week workshop, the sensational aspect of the telepathic exchange I was experiencing began to diminish, and the reality of this two-way conversation began to dawn. I returned to my home in San Diego and continued to maintain contact with The Nine. Instant access to answered questions and solved problems, made my Libra quality of indecision, a thing of the past !

A SUPPORT GROUP

As a counselling psychologist, I had spent ten years working with abused and delinquent children. My skills were optimized during supportive, individual counselling sessions with clients. Now, the interactions with The Nine were inspiring me to use my skills in a new way. I had a growing desire to contact open-minded people, form a weekly group, and explore our extra-sensory perceptions and potentials. Was anyone else experiencing this psychic communication?

I moved to Florida where I represented the state government, protecting abused children in the courts and counselling them and their families. In the conservative communities of northern Florida, I put an ad in the newspaper, my phone number and my wish to form a 'Spiritual Awareness' group. Seven people responded.

We began to meditate and talk, inspiring and supporting each other in our decisions to re-evaluate our cultural programming, and consider alternate ways of expressing the many untapped aspects of ourselves. Beneath our stretching and reaching was a growing desire to understand ourselves as spiritual beings in a materialistic world... a world that could no longer support its ideology of greed and power-over-others.

Yet what could we do? A mere handful of simple people living without power and greed, yet somehow enveloped in it.

It is an indication of the strong fiber of inner wisdom that existed in all of the small gatherings of awakening people at that time, that in the face of many obstacles and seemingly impossible life changes they persisted in the dark to meet, share and hope for the Light of a New Age.

It is easy now to look back and realize how much we were moved by faith in those early days, and to marvel at the psychic pioneers who preceded us in the work. They were even more alone than we were. They were strengthened by their contacts with people on other planets who knew what was ahead for us if we chose to enter the realms of expanded awareness.

A NEW NAME

Perhaps my awareness was stimulated in 1976 when I changed my name to Ocean. Recently divorced, living alone for the first time, attending college at night, and in need of a job to support myself, I began work as a Sales-Service Coordinator for a battery manufacturer in Santa Ana, California. An activist in the Women's Rights Movement while attending daytime classes at California State University, Fullerton, I carried that humanitarian purpose into my new life. I quickly noticed that the corporation where I now spent my time favored my male co-workers.

I was given a desk among the overworked secretaries, and soon was being asked to 'type' and 'run copies' by the predominantly male staff. Being conscientious about fulfilling my own job-description which required hours of telephone sales, I found the additional demands on my time to be excessive and demeaning. It was especially taxing since the men seemed to have time to swap stories in their offices, play golf, and go out for prolonged lunches. I was further frustrated in successful sales work when my patiently cultivated customers became seriously interested in placing a large order, and were then referred by the receptionist to the men for 'clinching' the deal.

I quickly realized that the complicated surname of my ex-husband added to the dilemma since customers could not remember nor pronounce my name. It was in the interest of simplifying my name, and choosing a name with no male lineage, that I made the decision to change my name. My rationale for choosing the name Ocean.... it was the first name that came to me. It was easy to spell, easy for other people to remember, unusual, and it went well with my first name.

And so my life as Joan Ocean began. I felt empowered by the simplicity of the name and enjoyed identifying myself on the telephone. My sales increased greatly. After receiving a million dollar order, I resigned from this company that had resisted in multiple ways my entry into its all male domain. I no longer needed to prove myself to them or me.

I am understanding cosmic messages more quickly these days, but then, it took me seven years before I understood the significance of my life in relation to my chosen name, Ocean !

MEETING JOHN

In 1978 I met Dr. John C. Lilly, the scientist who pioneered research in dolphin communication and isolation tanks. I felt a deep brotherly love for him. He nicknamed me "Seven Seas" in deference to my last name; and I affectionately called him "Cunningham" because that is his middle name and he is such a 'ham,' not to mention cunning ! I attended a workshop with John and his wife, Toni, in Montana. It had been advertised as a chance to converse with John about his altered consciousness experiences, but apparently John and Toni were much more interested in talking about dolphins. Every morning they gathered the participants together by playing dolphin vocalizations on a tape recorder. Every night I dreamed of dolphins and whales, without acknowledging anything more than a growing affection for them based on John's stories.

I didn't know it then, but they were to be a significant part of my future.

2
THE WHALE STORY

One bright, Sunday afternoon in late July, 1984, I was sitting outdoors when a friend came to my home to visit and introduce me to Jean-Luc Bozzoli. Jean-Luc, a visionary artist of French origin, and a resident of Australia, was travelling the California coast in a van enroute to Canada. He had been invited to join a small group of people interested in communicating with whales. The group was "Interspecies Communication," a non-profit organization founded by Jim Nollman. Jim was known in his field as a sensitive musician-scientist who had spent the last ten years using music to communicate with various species of animals. The group planned to spend thirty days in the wild with Killer Whales, the largest of the dolphin species, better known as Orcas.

Having no previous experience in that field, I responded enthusiastically but without personal involvement. I had no time for such excursions. My life and my future plans revolved around my career as a counselling psychologist at a Women's Health Center near San Francisco.

A HIGHER CALLING

A few days later, Jean-Luc phoned me from Washington to say an opening on the Orca trip had unexpectedly become available and he invited me to fill the space. I'd need to fly immediately to Seattle, as they were planning to disembark to the islands west of British Columbia in four days.

Somewhere within me, a dormant spark of adventure made the spontaneous decision and I said "Yes."

Winging my way north, I had my first chance to think rationally about my decision. Waves of insecurity swept over me as I considered what I had done ! Here I was flying to a primitive island, inhabited only by bears, to live in a tent and on a boat for a month with a group of people I didn't even know. What had come over me?

Trying to focus on the bright side, I envisioned this adventure as a vacation on a lovely uninhabited beach. I was in need of a change from the intensity of counselling women who were making decisions about abortions and incest. Getting away from it all was a greatly needed respite. It didn't matter that I had no ocean experience and I didn't even know how to swim. I convinced myself that the opportunity to commune with nature was the most appealing offer I could have.

Perhaps all those morning meditations of expanded consciousness were working, for this wonderful opportunity to offer itself to me ! Or, perhaps it was time for me to meet the whales....

WELCOME TO LONELINESS

Nine of us left Seattle on an early August morning. I traveled in a van with Jean-Luc. We were two of four people who had been 'volunteered' to paddle the kayaks from the Canadian mainland to the northern Pacific islands. The rest of the group were to arrive on a 42-foot yacht with all the supplies.

I had never kayaked before, but the eight-hour journey was exactly what my body and spirit needed. As I glided across the glass-blue ocean, awed by the green mountains looming on all sides of me, I sang American Indian chants and filled my lungs with the fresh sea air. There was not a whale in sight. And I breathed a sigh of relief !

At the end of the journey, the voluminous grey clouds rolled in and a cold drizzle which I would soon learn to expect in that northern climate, cast an eerie, unwelcoming appearance on the thickly forested island mountains. There was no sandy beach for relaxing in the sun, only an uneven shoreline strewn with rocks and huge logs that had drifted on the tide from the northern logging companies.

Pulling the kayak high on the rocky shore, I searched in the misty dusk for a level patch of dirt for my flimsy tent. The island was terribly inhospitable in the rain... a huge mountain of closely grown fir trees, moldy and decayed in their perennial moisture.

Feeling overcome with fatigue and loneliness, I stumbled my way back to the water's edge, climbing over the slippery, rolling logs. Pulling my all-weather jacket tighter around me, as if to insulate myself from the cheerless environment, I stood silently, gazing at the vast expanse of white-tipped ocean water that is the Johnstone Strait, and wondered why I had come.

For thirty days I would be here ! It seemed interminable. Already my clothes were damp and threatening mildew. The batteries for my flashlight were defunct without ever being used. The goals of this Orca communication trip included relating to our natural setting, to be in silence and repose... yet everyone seemed to be organizing themselves into task masters and work details.

I felt alienated from the people, and from this harsh setting. Sinking deeply into a gloom that matched the low-hanging clouds, I stared with unseeing eyes at the horizon, trying to escape my tiredness and doubts. I gazed without thought at the hypnotic whitecaps of the sea.

A LOVE SO STRONG

Suddenly I noticed an unusual movement in the distant waters. I reluctantly blinked out of my reverie to adjust my vision and focus on the aberration. There appeared to be some large form moving through the water. It looked like a submarine, partially submerged. Hoping it was the mysterious Orca whale, I blinked again, and concentrated my attention.

No, I could see it was not an Orca... no telltale fin cutting the water, no flash of white on black. I watched as the huge submerged form moved hypnotically and with purpose through the water towards me.

Finally, I identified it, and a warm glow of recognition passed over me as I silently transmitted a greeting. It was a WHALE, but not an Orca.

It was a California Gray Whale, the only species of whale I had ever seen before.

What was the whale of my home state doing here, in these waters where whalers had decimated its population decades ago? The questions left my mind as I watched, entranced by the fluid progress of this solitary mammoth of the sea. Forward it slowly swam, moving towards me into the shallow, pebbled water. As I watched in amazement, the mighty bulk began to roll in the shallows, so close to me I could have touched it had I moved into the icy waters. The whale rolled once, then stopped at an odd angle, an angle that left one of its gentle moist eyes gazing intently at me. I stared back, and in that moment a great flood of well-being and acceptance swept over me. I was instantly filled with a love so strong and so deep that I felt my body would disintegrate from an inability to contain it.

This is the meaning of Truth, I thought. Now I know what is meant by 'Truth' and 'Beauty.'

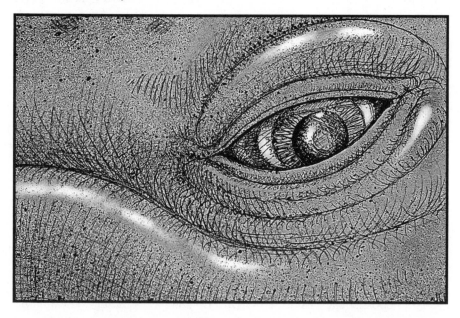

As waves of deep peace swept over my awareness, I felt my heart open to the whale and I felt an exchange of immediate, total knowing pass between us. I was completely enfolded in a soft bubble of wisdom and love.

Within a few moments, I began to feel that the intensity of this bonding was so strong I could no longer contain it... surely my heart would burst ! And as that thought entered my awareness, the waves of love instantly ceased, and I found myself in my normal cognitive realm again.

In that moment, I understood that the whale was experiencing my emotions, and it knew when to diminish the intensity of our interaction. The whale had responded to my thoughts and feelings.

As my heart filled with joy, I understood I was receiving the love for humanity and all living things... that is the deep spirituality of the whale. Our bonding was an immersion into my open-hearted gratitude and the natural loving presence of this being.

I felt very humble. My first communication with a whale had occurred, and with such impact that my doubts of only minutes before were now transformed into great anticipation for the days ahead.

I was also infused with warmth and appreciation for the diligent, mindful members of Interspecies Communication*, who were including me as a participant in this great adventure.

THE MESSAGE

During those thirty days at the edge of the ocean, on a thickly forested island, living in a tent, I had many hours to be alone with nature. I had little opportunity to do that in my past, and my body and spirit absorbed the blessed silence of that lonely island. It was nourishing and nurturing.

I began to write many messages I found on my mind... messages to myself, messages about changes in the physical structures of humans and their genetic memories. I didn't always understand it, but I recorded it all. There seemed to be a connection between this information and the close proximity of the whales in the waters around that island.

---

*For those of you who would like to hear some of our musical interactions with the Orca Whales, I recommend you purchase the Interspecies Communication, Inc. cassette tape, *Orca's Greatest Hits* (Appendix). It's a classic.

As I began to realize that this 'vacation' with the Orcas had more significance than I had originally anticipated, I began to ask more directed questions while I sat in a row boat or on a log on the shore. When I posed the question about my growing interest in cetaceans, and about their role in general on the planet, the answers flowed smoothly from my pen:

Question: "In what ways can work with dolphins and whales serve Creation and mankind?"

Response: "These mammals are here to be of service in Earth's evolution. They bring with them many ancient memories and advanced technical knowledge. The biases of earthlings have prevented acceptance of dolphin knowledge until this time. There are many scientists and individuals including those in your own government, who are aware of this intelligence, and yet have not been able to reveal it to the general population. The egos of the masses will not permit acceptance of this infinite knowledge from creatures of the sea.

However, the time is drawing near when human ears will be opened to this reality. There is much preparation to be done. There is a need for sensitive humans to interact with the cetaceans and bring this knowledge to the populace in a manner that will ensure acceptance.

There is no doubt that you can assist in this endeavor if this is your choice. Your natural affinity with the energies of nature and the ocean will contribute to the expansion of human-dolphin communication. Your acknowledgment of beauty and order drew you to this project. Your connections to the Atlantean vibrations and those of ancient Egypt are filling your awareness due to the similarity of vibrations being radiated to Earth at this time.

These are the Energies of the Dolphins and Whales. We would like you to come play and interact with us. We have been aware of your energies in Florida and California.

Our wisdom is that of the past and of the future. We have been joyously awaiting this time of evolution for the planet, sending our healing rays to the earth, assisting those who are aware of us, and soon, to release to the sensitives of the Golden Age, the wisdom of the Ancients. The time is quickly approaching when humans will have ears to hear this knowledge, and will begin to benefit from it. This information comes as Truth and Beauty. It is the information of Love. It is a combination of technical-scientific data with the vibrations of Universal Love. In your world these aspects have been separated.

We now return knowledge to wholeness. The knowledge of telepathy, history, transportation, and unknown energy sources are but a few of the intelligences that we shall communicate to you, and in fact have been communicating to some of you for hundreds of years.

We serve as inspiration for many and we are your teachers on planet Earth. Come learn from us and play with us. For our means of teaching is through joy and trust. You respond to our love and light, for you are also a Being of Truth and Beauty. All is in perfect order and when the time is proper, humankind will receive the full breadth of our knowledge.

We thank you for calling upon us. We radiate our love and light to blend and interact with yours in Peace."

I shared this message with only three people on the Orca trip. It was new, special, and I felt too sensitive about the material to share it with everyone.

TELEPATHY

In this channeling, the word telepathy was used, but it seemed an inadequate noun to express the holographic communication that the cetaceans were transmitting and I was translating. This further description of this word then presented itself:

> *"The vibrational exchange you refer to as 'telepathy' is expanded to mean an exchange of radiations between cetaceans and humans which then creates a new and more perfect image-tone in its fusion. An original, unique thought-form, rather than a sharing of already known thoughts."*

Over the years, as my contacts with dolphins increased, I found this definition to be an apt description of our interactions with each other. Being with dolphins and whales in any possible intimate circumstances led to a blending of feelings and ideas that produced new mind-sets, new ways of understanding life, new projects that were stimulated by art and an appreciation of beauty and nature, rather than the old incentives of business and money.

CHANGES

I soon began questioning all the old paradigms of conducting business, of making money and being successful. I knew there was a better, more creative, more harmonic way for people and groups to interact and produce a finished product that exceeded anything done before, and that fulfilled the needs of the participants and of their role as guardians of the earth.

The channeled message indicated I could be a 'dolphin and whale ambassador' if I chose to be. Until then I had been a counselling psychologist. Well, now it was up to me. What did I want to do? Did I want to change? What could my background in therapy have to do with cetaceans?

Soon I was to understand that connection.

The island breathes
as its lush tropical undergrowth births multiple life forms.
Within our cells,
the memory of the Original Vibration
merges with our pulsating Earth. Through Love,
we converge with the Creative Forces.
In harmony with wave lengths that predominate in the universe,
we enter the gateway to another dimension.
Embracing the Spirit of our Source,
we become an expression of it.

3

MEETING THE DOLPHINS

fter spending the month of August with the Orca whales, Jean-Luc and I began travelling by car through California and the Southwest sharing a presentation of guided meditation and audio-visuals of Jean-Luc's extraordinary artwork projected onto a screen. We called the presentation the "Dolphin Connection."

It was a journey of love, and we revealed the fulfillment we experienced in this sharing by expressing the joy in our hearts to all the wonderful people who came to hear our stories and see our visuals. Our spiritual purposes and realizations were the impetus in our mutual life path.

During a presentation of the Dolphin Connection show, I met a new friend, Roxanne Kremer, who has invested her life and money in helping the Pink Dolphins of the Amazon River. They are an endangered species. She was about to leave for Peru to document in film their precarious situation. I had been dreaming about pink dolphins, without knowing they actually existed. When Roxanne invited me to join her group, I immediately said, "Yes."

As part of our journey to Peru, we stopped in Florida to meet with the people of the Dolphin Research Center in Grassy Key. It was there I had my first encounter in the water with dolphins. The following story was recorded immediately after my experience.

THE FIRST TIME

The dolphins are calling me to come and play. They nod their heads and chatter and smile. They dive below and flip their tails. They are provocative and irresistible.

And so I slowly lower myself into the cool, salty water that is churning from their activity. This is a new experience, and water is not my element. I hold on to the floating dock. Immediately three dolphins surround me, and I impulsively reach out to touch them, longing to feel their silken skin.

A quick caress is all they allow before they dive down and invite me to follow.

I release my grip on the security of the dock and move out into the water. Now they are all around... happy to see me in their midst, inviting me to swim with them. I feel their joy. It's contagious. It encompasses me, permeating my awareness until it is all that I know.

Laughing like a child, I am completely attentive to my new friends. Together we spin and splash and swirl. The dolphins come from all directions. Now below me, now behind, now surfacing in front, gazing at me with their all-knowing eyes, vying for attention. I hug them and hold them, slipping and sliding away from their bodies, feeling their power and coordination, their sonar and sounds.

As I tread water, one dolphin moves his dorsal fin to my hand. I quickly hold on, and I am taken for an exhilarating ride through the choppy ocean. I am flying ! I experience it over and over again. I am completely involved in the moment, laughing joyously and wanting more. The dolphins appear to feel the same way. They never tire or swim away. They weave in and out among themselves, speaking in clicks to gain my attention. They read my reactions with their sonar sensors, and within their watery world we play for hours... loving each other, loving our lives, and knowing that land and water can no longer separate us. We are all part of the same wonderful environment, united in joy and appreciation.

PEACE SURROUNDS ME

When I climbed out of the water after spending two hours with the dolphins, I felt very quiet. Every movement I made was flowing like warm honey. A deep sense of peace surrounded me, and the world appeared vibrant and unusually beautiful.

I was very aware of all sounds, sights and smells. Loud sounds startled me and I felt delicate and vulnerable in the gentle breezes. I noticed a soggy plastic bag floating near a boat in the water, and I became very concerned. Plastic bags were often floating in the water near boats, but now I recognized it as a danger for the sea life. I insisted on taking a hooked pole from a boat and removing the bag.

I became aware of every living thing... to the extent of being careful not to step on the occasional ant that was hurrying by on the wooden sidewalk.

EMPATHIC UNDERSTANDING

While swimming with the dolphins, volumes of information about the interdependence of the oceans and the earth had filled my awareness. I understood how carefully ecosystems were intertwined and related, and how every living thing has a purpose.

I experienced a symbiotic love for the ocean. I felt protective of it. I accepted completely my personal connection to it, and my responsibility to preserve and respect all of the vast life forms that resided within it.

This information came to me by 'absorption.' It was not intellectualized, it was not visualized in words or images, it was felt. It was in some way absorbed into the fabric of my intelligence so that whatever previous knowledge existed within me was incorporated into the new information and the ultimate understandings involved my knowledge and the knowledge of the cetaceans.

In this particular case, my knowledge of the ocean was minimal, while my feelings of love and joy were optimal. The knowledge from the dolphins regarding the ocean was extensive, and when it combined with my feelings of love, the result was a feeling of love for the ocean, based on a newly acquired empathic understanding of it.

BEING OPEN TO RECEIVE

This description of my interactions with the cetaceans and my communications with them, is not unique. I believe many people have had this same experience. It appears to be an exchange of information that occurs when we humans are open to receive it. The way I experience being open to receive, is when I am enjoying playing with the dolphins or watching the whales so intently that my concentration is totally involved with them. I am not distracted by anything else. In fact, my thinking seems to be disengaged, and I am only feeling and enjoying. Perhaps I could say that I am 'in the moment.' It is not contrived nor planned, it is a natural outcome of the deep feelings of love I have in their company, which makes me focus on them and nothing else. It is a very spontaneous and natural reaction to their enthralling presence.

A WONDROUS GIFT

One day, while swimming with captive dolphins in the Florida Keys, a female dolphin swam directly towards me, and sharply bumped my abdomen with her beak. It startled me, and I decided to leave the ocean-enclosure, thinking it an act of aggression.

The dolphin however, did not seem agitated; but chattered with a provocative behavior that I recognized as an invitation to come and play.

Feeling no fear or doubt, I immediately returned to the water, curious about her intentions. She slowly and easily proceeded to swim time after time, directly toward my body, giving me very firm jolts, one after another along five vertical points in the center of my body, hitting me from my navel, upward to my neck. Instinctively, I ducked my head under water, and the dolphin made her final contact with the center of my forehead, butting it strongly and abruptly, before swimming away.

As I floated alone in the quiet water, I became aware of a physical reaction in my body that felt like an electrical current moving from the base of my spine upward to the top of my head. It seemed like a very warm voltage of rising energy, relative to the cool afternoon water that surrounded me.

I remained quietly in the water for a while. My ever-analytical mind searching for a rational explanation for this phenomena I was experiencing. There was none.

Shakily I climbed out of the ocean pool, feeling light headed, less aware of my body as a physical weight, and more aware of it as an energy body that was free-flowing. It seemed as though more and more oxygen was filling my body with each breath I took, and as if some blocks had been released, allowing my breath to flow unobstructed now.

Six friends were waiting to take me to a restaurant. As usual after being with dolphins, we were in very mellow moods and there was no need for words. Besides, I couldn't imagine telling them about that unusual experience. As I mulled it over in my mind, it even sounded silly to me. So I said nothing, until we were seated around a table for dinner.

Then, much to my surprise, my friend Suzanne began to quietly tell me about an experience she had that day while in the water, that seemed to be an activation, by a dolphin, of her seven chakras. I was incredulous as I listened to her softly relating to me a replication of my own experience. She was similarly amazed when she heard me say I had experienced the same thing. We then asked the other five people at the table if they had had any similar interaction. No one else had, and they had no explanation for our contact which resembled experiences of kundalini energy moving along the spine to the crown chakra, balancing the energy body as it rises.

Understanding that it was unnecessary to translate the healing into words, we accepted it as a wondrous gift.

I am quite sure the dolphins help each other in that way. One look at their sleek forms makes you feel they are healthy indeed. Healing is second nature, and part of their play !

THE AMAZON

During the weeks on the Amazon River we observed the small grey and the pink dolphins in their natural habitat. They seemed to escort our wooden boat, as we floated down the river filming the shoreline and the acres of barren land where jungles had once thrived.

It was very hot in that tropical climate, and the mosquitos were excited about our presence ! So, admittedly I had more than one reason for looking forward to a dip in the water. The dolphins had been quietly escorting us downriver, about fifteen feet behind our boat. From time to time they would disappear and then surface again, in front of us. Their behavior, more sedate than bottlenose dolphins, consisted of rolling leisurely just below the surface and eyeing us through the muddy brown water.

As soon as Roxanne indicated that it was appropriate to enter the river, I was the first one in. Glad to enjoy the relative coolness of the water, I paddled around for a while before I began to observe my surroundings.

One of the local river people was in a dug-out canoe, close to shore. Since he was fishing, I was careful to avoid his area of the river. The dolphins had moved further upstream, but they appeared to be curious about us and they remained within sight of our cameras.

Floating leisurely in a life jacket, I became aware of a repetitive splashing sound. I looked over in its direction. I noticed the fisherman leaning over his boat, holding his pole in one hand and slapping the water with his other.

Thinking this to be very curious, I called to our Spanish speaking translator to ask if he knew why the local Indian man was doing this. He conversed with the local Indian, back and forth, until finally he turned to me with his answer: "The man is fishing for Piranha. He entices them to his fishing line by splashing the water."

In one minute I was back on our boat, suddenly noticing that no one else was swimming in the Amazon !

I relate this story for a few different reasons. For one, it's funny. For another, it's an example of what not to do when you visit dolphins in new locations. And mainly because, as that journey in Peru continued, I returned to the water and swam regularly whenever the dolphins were in view. Apparently the Amazon Dolphins eat Piranha, and I felt very safe in their presence.

I WANT TO BE A DOLPHIN !

Swimming with dolphins in the water began to bring about noticeable changes in me. More and more, I wanted to be like them ! I wanted to be a dolphin ! Now this was strange. I had a large house, rooms full of furniture, many friends at home, and a fulfilling career. Why did I want to be a dolphin?

They were having so much fun. And I became like a child in their presence. None of the recreational activities or vacations I'd experienced in the past had provided this much relaxation and enjoyment. This experience was creative and healthy, and it introduced me to an entirely new realm of existence... the water world. It was like being on another planet... only better.

I had the name of Ocean for seven years, but did not know the ocean, except that it represented peace, and I enjoyed looking at it. Now I became aware of the ocean. A wonderful mysterious environment I had never explored, and that held untold adventures for me.

At every opportunity I would immerse myself into this watery world, trying to sink into the feelings and sensations of the aquatic creatures that resided there. Listening to the sounds, experiencing the touch of the water on my skin, so much more tangible than air. What is it like to be weightless and buoyant? To move within the changing currents of water, to feel the earth turn, to slide on the waves, and be surrounded by the varied and unique concerts of sea animals. To play in the sparkling shafts of sunlight and bubbles, to feel the pull of the moon and the stars, to hear the pebbles rolling in the surf, and the generators of giant ships, to talk with and know your friends who are miles away, to own no possessions, to dive to 800 feet, to have seventy percent of the planet as your intimate and cozy home, and then to pass through the surface of your reality to soar into another air-breathing world and gaze at the species there, just for your own entertainment !

I loved floating face down in the ocean, breathing silently and gazing at the unending blueness all around. And then, eventually, learning to dive and coast deep along the sandy bottom making believe I could remain there forever.

Back on land, I began to notice subtle changes in my thoughts. I wanted to travel freely in the world. I wanted to meet people of every culture, in diverse environments. I wanted to share my stories, and see if other people in other countries felt the way I did. I wanted to simplify my life, remove the weight of all the things I owned, all the bills, all the hectic schedules, to swim unimpeded in the world, and see what would happen. Just thinking about doing that, made me feel great !

In addition to a growing desire to know the world and its inhabitants, something else had been kindled. I began to understand my connection to the organic macrocosm known as Earth. Contact with the cetaceans had developed a compassion in me for the Earth, as well as the ocean. A feeling that related them in a personal way, to my own body and to my life.

CELLULAR MEMORIES

What had happened? I believe at least two processes had occurred: the dolphins had projected information into me through feelings... and had stimulated feelings and knowledge that already existed in the cells of my body, in the mind in my cells, in my cells' memories.

We experienced a meeting of mutual empathy, and in that meeting I sensed a familiarity with their particular wavelength. Their communications resonated with the telepathic communications in the 1970s with The Nine of Sirius B. When I inquired about this similarity, I received the following message:

"The star system Sirius radiates a high frequency of Light and is a stabilizing force in the galaxy. Because of its intensity and constancy, it is a useful vibration to interact with dark planets or those which are very dense. Therefore, it was decided that the Sirius energies could assist the Earth in its evolutionary growth by interacting with the Earth patterns, and elevating the vibrations or adding more Light. To do this without creating solar imbalances, Sirius entities were incarnated on Earth and in that way, brought their radiant energies to assist in Earth's evolvement.

The properties and frequencies of the oceans were more conducive to assimilating the Sirius frequencies than any other area of the planet.

The Sirian Beings were able to travel to and from their planet through certain vibrational diagrams within the oceans. These are the entities you have experienced within the ocean. The dolphins are at one with these energies, and although the present dolphins are not pure Sirian energies, they retain the knowledge and the memories of the ancient inhabitants of Earth who were ocean beings.

The dolphins also interact with vibrational patterns that still access the Space Sister/Brotherhood and other high-frequency Beings to your planet. By remaining in contact with these planetary vortex centers, and by retaining their awareness of themselves as beings of Light, the dolphins do carry the vibrations of Sirius and other Celestial Radiations; and do thereby serve as catalysts for these light waves which continue to be very healing and nourishing for your planet.

As humans increase their ability to perceive and receive Light, they also begin to experience these ancient vibrations carried by the dolphins, and still present in specific pockets, so to speak, of the planet.

The vibrations of Sirius were a formative Ray upon this planet, and remain very active within the Earth's vibratory field at this time."

More and more, with each passing day, I looked forward to the unfolding story that now inspired my understanding and direction.

Caring for sacred spaces in the jungle,
the Amazon River Dolphins
reflect a vision of appreciation in their smile...
accessing realms that resonate compatibly with the rain forest.
With resplendent colorforms,
they create harmonic realities
that ripple through the universal mind integrating us
with the magic of nature.

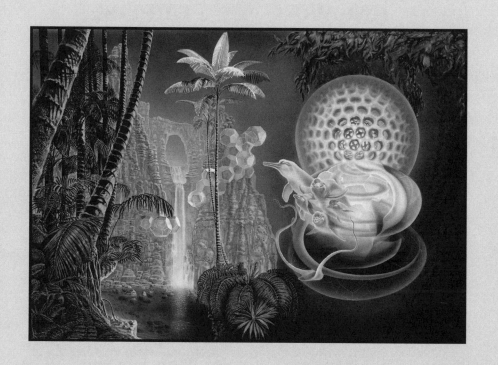

4
KNOWING MY PURPOSE

In the wisdom gained by my contact with the cetaceans and their ocean environment, I began to understand that every life form on Earth has a reason for existing; whether it is to add beauty to our world, or to add oxygen, or knowledge toward progress in our evolution. With that realization, I began to wonder how I could contribute. What was my purpose in being alive right now? Why was I here?

Have you ever asked that question? I began asking it of everyone I met, if I thought they had any inside information on that age-old subject. No one had an answer for me.

One day, I sat down with a piece of paper and wrote the question to the dolphins. As my hand began to quickly record an answer, I was reminded *"... that our planet is a place of great beauty and diversity. It has more varieties of colors and life forms than any other planet known in the Universe. There are colorful birds, fish, and flowers. There are diverse climates and terrains. It is a planet of free choice, and we have been offered many possible choices."*

So often we no longer see its beauty. And because we are not seeing the Beauty, we are not expressing our appreciation. It is the expression or feeling of appreciation that feeds the beauty on our planet. In multiple ways, the absence of gratitude in our world results in the demise of our planet. Expressing heartfelt gratitude is one of our intrinsic purposes, a sacred responsibility.

And when I asked, "How can I help the Earth?" the accelerated writing revealed this message:

"Be. Be Fully Who You Are.

You have become very immersed in the programming of your life style. You remain in a role you've been taught by your loved ones, your culture and your environment.

You are truly meant to be much more than that.

You are not merely a female, or an American citizen, or an Earth citizen, you are a being of the Universe. You are created from a vibration of Love. You are a pulsating ray of Light in a physical body. In this Light you can become all things. You are not limited. Why restrict yourself to one career, one location, one planet?

Be fully who you are.

And when you accept your fullness, you are no longer adversely affected by situations or people that at one time created stress in your life. Time-consuming, earthbound concerns will no longer monopolize your life. Your spirit becomes free to acknowledge your true profession, your true work; and to become aware of capabilities you don't even know that you have. Release all of the earthbound problems, and see them for what they are: activities created by you, to avoid contact with your higher self, your unlimited self.

Make a decision now, to gently remove all unnecessary work and interruptions from your life. Free yourself so that the fullness of who you really are, can flourish."

I automatically passed this message through my intuitive sensing (censoring) devices, and I understood it as true. I decided to follow its advice.

I began to do the things I enjoyed doing, and being with the people who were magic and fun. I chose to eat foods that I craved and to live in environments that were beautiful and enriching. Some of these decisions cost money initially, so I used the money from the sale of my furniture.

Many of my new choices ran head-long into deeply ingrained fears that threatened to deter me. These were fears about 'security' and my 'future'. What would happen to me when I grew old? I was a single woman now, didn't I need to plan for my future? What if I became incapacitated some day? What if? What if?

In the final decision-making process, the prevailing question was: did I want to forfeit living a full life now, in fear of vague and negative possibilities in my 'future?' And wasn't this type of fearful thinking a game I participated in with the rest of society... as a means of avoiding living responsibly in the present?

I decided not to let lack of money stop me, nor anything else. Ultimately, we are each responsible to ourselves for our actions, and the best we can do is to contact that God-self within us and respond to that inner voice.

Our purpose during this lifetime is to use our gifts to support and strengthen each other, our Earth, and all living things. When we use our skills with knowledge for the benefit of humanity, we are fulfilling our purpose.

Besides, the dolphins were beckoning me...

5
TELEMPATHY

Often I have heard people remarking about the sense of safety they feel in the water with the dolphins. What is it about the presence of dolphins that creates a field of well-being and peace of mind? Even among people who one moment before had looked at these 400 pounds of seven-foot long muscle and vowed never to get into the water with them. Then miraculously, in the water surrounded by dolphins, all fear vanishes; even when fear may be wise, due to choppy water or unusually boisterous dolphin behaviors. In some inexplicable way, the dolphins' bio-electric field radiates a sense of security. They are not threatening, and our irrational fears are alleviated.

Recently, Jean-Luc and I visited an art gallery in Lahaina, Hawaii to talk about publishing Jean-Luc's latest paintings as posters. We met with the art dealer in his office and showed him our previous publications of visionary notecards. As the impeccably dressed, well-spoken art expert turned our notecard over to read the inspirational message on the back of the card, Jean-Luc and I exchanged a knowing smile and silently waited for the reaction by this man to the channeling from the dolphins. He read the entire message before looking up and asking incredulously if I had really been in contact with dolphins. When I responded positively, he then lowered his voice and began to share a story he had not related to anyone before.

DOLPHINS LEND SUPPORT

Although living in Hawaii, he took very little time to be outdoors. Since he had previously enjoyed swimming, he decided to resume a daily swim program. He chose to complete a one mile swim from the mainland of Maui to a small nearby island reef.

After swimming for half a mile he became extremely tired and dismayed because his strength was ebbing so quickly. He stopped swimming for a while to decide whether to continue swimming to the reef or to return to the mainland, each direction being a half mile away. Then to compound matters he looked toward the waters ahead and saw groups of black fins cutting the water, moving towards him.

Immediately, he thought, "Sharks!" But that thought was quickly followed by the realization that the arched swimming behavior was indicative of dolphins, not sharks.

He relaxed a little, and choosing to continue to swim forward, he became aware that the dolphins had reached him and were now all around him in great numbers. As he continued to swim, the dolphins stayed with him, changing their previous direction to escort him in the water.

Suddenly, a very unusual feeling came over him as he looked into the water and saw dolphins swimming beneath him in perfect synchronistic movements with his own swim strokes. Looking to both sides, he noticed the dolphins that surrounded him were also moving in time with his own movements, slowing their pace to swim side by side with him.

He then became aware that his tiredness had vanished, and he was easily swimming forward to the reef ahead. He felt something very significant had happened. At the same time, his rational mind was struggling to accept it.

Now, he asked me, could that have been true? Did the dolphins swim directly to him and lend their support in a way that provided so much additional energy that the swim to the island and back to Maui was sheer delight?

Even though he had experienced it, he was still having difficulty relating it to his current belief system. It was with great relief that he listened to a confirmation of his experience by Jean-Luc and myself.

ALTRUISTIC DOLPHINS

I have had numerous similar experiences of feeling energized and strengthened by the presence of dolphins. When I swam in the Amazon River in Peru, I learned that the water was teeming with Piranha, and yet I felt very safe when the dolphins were escorting me, or simply observing me. It is surprising to me to feel that sense of safety with dolphins, because for years I had a debilitating fear of water. In the Soviet Union, Dr. Igor Charkovsky in his pioneering work with underwater birthing, has shown that infants can remain contentedly in the Black Sea for up to twenty-four hours as long as dolphins are present. (Addendum)

Recently, in Australia, a seventeen-year old boy was saved by dolphins when a shark attacked his surfboard. The dolphins kept the shark at bay, while the injured boy, assisted by his friends, climbed back onto his board and caught the next wave into shore. The boys and witnesses said they had no doubt that the dolphins had saved his life.[*]

There are many stories of dolphins saving humans from drowning and of whales leading boats into safe harbors (*Mind in the Waters*, Joan McIntyre). In these stories, the cetaceans seem to appear from nowhere, sometimes in the midst of a vast ocean, to assist the human in distress. How do they know the human needs help? What do they hear or feel in the water? What message does their echo-locating system transmit to them?

DOLPHINS' RESPONSE ABILITY

I have mentioned some of the experiences in which I received wisdom from the cetaceans. Now, what about times when they were receiving information from me? In addition to the Gray Whale interaction in the northern Pacific, I have had other experiences with dolphins that contribute to my feelings of empathic-telepathic exchange while in the water with them. Whether we are in Monkey Mia, Australia, the Gulf of Mexico, or Lahaina, Hawaii.

[*] The Sun News, Melbourne, Australia, January 4, 1989.

I remember my first experience with the captive dolphins in the Keys of Florida. Without knowing how to do much more than desperately tread water, I reached out to the dolphins and they pulled me along behind them as I held on to their dorsal fin. After circling around for a while with much laughter and exuberance, one dolphin dove while I was still holding on to him. I had the presence of mind to close my mouth, then quickly thought, "Oh my gosh, I can't breathe. I can't hold my breath !" Instantly the dolphin brought me to the surface ! It felt very much as though he had changed his direction when he perceived my feelings.

Later, when I was prepared for the dive and held my breath, the dolphin remained underwater for a longer time until I again thought, "Uh oh ! I'm running out of air." I depended on the dolphin to surface with me. I didn't want to let go and rise to the surface on my own. The dolphin seemed to sense this and took responsibility for my next breath.

I mention this as an example of what happened to me in my naivete during the first swims with dolphins. I do not recommend expecting the dolphins to be responsible for our safety. It's important that we remain responsible for ourselves. I do think the dolphins are often sensitive to the frailties and needs of other species, and when they choose to, they respond in a helpful way.

CAPTIVE DOLPHINS

Conversely, I have some reservations about recommending captive dolphin swims to people. One day at a captive facility, a large 500 pound dolphin came from behind me, pushed me against the fence that separated him from the open ocean, and held me there, giving me a quick lesson about the strength and power of dolphins. The rusted fencing caused some lacerations on my arm, and a sudden fear gripped me as I realized the dolphin had totally immobilized me. Fortunately or purposely he had done so with my head above water. My experiences with domesticated dolphins some- times make me feel that the dolphins have learned some very unusual behaviors. But the lesson was well taken.

In October, 1984, I attended a Dolphin Council at Ojai Foundation in Ojai, California. John Lilly and a number of other people were talking about the future of two captive dolphins John had worked with for five years. Their names were Rosie and Joe, and they were being transported to Florida to await a decision about possible release to their original ocean environment. Marine Mammal Laws have strict regulations governing a request for release of dolphins.

Having heard so much about these two special dolphins, I looked forward to seeing them when I was invited to the Research Lab in Florida. Visiting the facility in December, 1984 I was saddened to hear that the dolphin baby Rosie recently birthed had died. Rosie seemed to be in mourning.

By invitation I entered the water with a pool of female dolphins, and enjoyed playing with them. I was very aware however, of Rosie keeping to herself on the far side of our enclosure. I belatedly wondered if my presence in the pool was inappropriate, because I began to feel an overwhelming sense of sadness. I climbed out of the water, and left to change my clothes.

A VERY SPECIAL DOLPHIN

Before leaving the Dolphin Center for the day, I stood on the training platform momentarily, watching Rosie in a small section of the pool, separating herself from all the other dolphins, and my heart went out to her. I felt a deep love and a wish to help her in some way.... yet I also felt a sense of hopelessness, because there was nothing I could do.

Silently I talked to myself, "Oh, Rosie, I wish I could comfort you, or help you in some way. I wish I could hold you and let you know that I really care about you."

With deep sadness in my heart, I watched her silently eyeing me from the other side, hardly moving in her little section of self-imposed exile.

Then quietly and slowly, she slid through the water towards me, coming directly across the pool from the other side. When she reached the platform where I was crouching down, close to the edge, she gently lifted her head and half her body up, out of the water near my feet, and remained in that position while I instinctively reached out and held her, caressing her skin with all the gentle and loving energy my hands and arms could exude.

It felt wonderful to make contact with her, and I experienced a strong emotional reaction of gratitude and affection. She then silently slid back down into the water and returned to her solitude in the distant section of the pool.

And as I watched her, I knew, she had done it for me. She had come over to me in response to my need. Oh, perhaps it was good for her too, but I knew that in the midst of her sorrow, she experienced my sorrow, and she gave to me the gift of herself, which brought me joy. There is no doubt about it. This is the love of a dolphin. This is the love of that particular dolphin.* And this was another example of a communication transmitted through empathic feelings.

ENTERING DOLPHIN CONSCIOUSNESS

My contacts with dolphins in rivers and oceans around the world led to a means of communicating that superseded the prevalent paradigm of linear thinking and verbalization. The communications seemed to be transmitted through feelings, but the experience included imagery and cognitions.

I experienced this empathic, total body exchange while swimming in the water with dolphins.

I wondered about the ingredients of this communication. What were the particular circumstances that facilitated its occurrence? The presence of a large body of water seemed obvious. Perhaps the experienced feelings were transmitted most clearly in a water setting.

I knew that the cetaceans were receiving my reactions and feelings because they responded to them immediately, I also felt that their wisdom was being transmitted to me with great clarity. I am not particularly clairvoyant, and yet their messages reached me on a level beyond rationalizations.

Their information seemed to infuse my cellular system and record understandings in me on an experiential basis. That is, it was as though I had <u>lived</u> <u>through</u> the events necessary to immerse myself into their life

---

* Rosie (and Joe too) are now free again in the ocean, thanks to the efforts of the Oceanic Research Communication Alliance (O.R.C.A.).

stories. It felt as though the cetaceans were exposing me to their actual oceanic experiences.

And yet why were these experiences so grounded in human understandings and belief systems? How could a message sent by the dolphins be so related to my experiences on planet Earth in 1985? They seemed to reflect my perspective, rather than the cognitions of an oceanic being. Where did my knowledge end and theirs begin? Or were they merely parroting into my awareness a wisdom I already possessed and had not known?

THE TELEPATHY OF EMPATHY

Then I remembered their explanation of our telepathic exchange. They said their telepathic communication was an exchange of information between cetaceans and humans that created a new and more perfect image-tone in its fusion. In other words, when humans and cetaceans chose to merge their thought-forms and feelings, the resulting information was a creative blending of the two. It was a combination of my knowledge and theirs. It was transmitted through empathy. Rather than telepathy, it is TELEMPATHY.

I believe dolphins communicate large quantities of information in very short periods of time. Knowledge that includes feelings, history, forecasts, and appropriate pertinent facts that apply to individuals personally. The information is alive and useful ! It pertains to the life and understandings of the receiver, because it is a mutual interaction based on the genetic data base of both or all communicators.

This aspect of mutual interaction and sharing of feelings, explains why some people receive one message from a particular dolphin, and someone else will receive what appears to be a conflicting message from that same dolphin. The dolphin messages are combining with the feelings of the individual. Sometimes these feelings are below the awareness of the individual. They may be longings that the individual is experiencing that are not even related to the interaction with the dolphin. This has led to confusion among some people who communicate with dolphins.

At first I thought the dolphins were playing with human feelings in the way they play in the water with each other. Then I quickly realized that our feelings and biased perceptions are coloring the transmissions. Our feelings and thoughts are being reflected back to us in the communications.

This is where our responsibility to be unbiased and nonjudgemental comes in. When there are no attachments to outcome, the communication is simple and clear.

On the part of the dolphins, there appear to be no hidden agendas. They communicate through feelings, through empathy or vibrational impulses. These wave lengths are different than language, in which information can be withheld, misinterpreted or colored by emotions.

The dolphin communications are very clear, without deceptions or secrets. They seem to transmit on a particular frequency I refer to as love or peace, and within those pure feelings, only truth is revealed and relayed. It is unadulterated intelligence that is a sharing of egalitarians at a global-universal level.

I am sure many of you have experienced this process yourself. If not with dolphins, perhaps in nature, while feeling on top of the world. It's a natural high ! It is an exchange that is felt in your heart, and grows out of love.

This was enough to make me want to spend as much time as possible in the water with the whales and dolphins. I was intrigued.

I had always been interested in supporting love and empathy in people. Now I was interested in bringing together groups of people with groups of dolphins. I had experienced some spontaneous people/cetacean interactions with friends, but I wanted to meet with specific people who had an interest in developing this human pod/dolphin pod communication with me.

This led to the Dolphin Ocean Swim projects in Hawaii. An organized program to facilitate a group bonding among a small group of people who would live together, share dolphin swims together and meditate together. The next chapter is about that experience.

6
DOLPHIN OCEAN SWIM

Rocking gently from side to side, I feel a sense of well-being that fills my heart. Life is perfect. I sit comfortably on a 40-foot catamaran named *U.F.O.* and watch the wide expanse of ocean surrounding me, containing eleven silent people bobbing on its teal blue undulations. They are oblivious to my watchful eyes, as they focus on the sleek, agile water beings that randomly encircle them. The dolphins have come to spend some time with us again, on another early morning along the Na Pali Coast of Hawaii.

Does my peace of mind originate from the presence of these intelligent and joyful cetaceans, or is it stimulated by the fulfillment that comes from providing an experience for my human friends that immediately removes all stress and tension from their thoughts and bodies? An experience that may affect them as it has me... filling them with joy, changing values and belief systems forever.

Just two months ago a recently retired friend, Sharina White and I decided to gather people together to participate in a group swim with dolphins. Our mutual excitement about the possibilities of this pioneering research into dolphin/human communication brought the idea into form in less than a month. Now, here we were with a group of interested people who had travelled to Hawaii from the mainland, USA, to open themselves to their dreams of interspecies communication with dolphins.

In my years of travelling to share personal dolphin stories with audiences in many countries, I had hundreds of requests from interested people to join me in my swims with dolphins. People who selflessly offered time and skills to assist me in my personal research. Many people who heard of my organization, the Dolphin Connection, thought I directed a dolphin facility with pools and captive dolphins as many researchers do. This was not my goal nor my focus. My contacts were with free-swimming dolphins and whales. The research was personal and unique. It was a re-search or a renewed search for ways of communicating that allowed the animal or mammal to be the teacher. It meant my willingness to remove as much as possible the old paradigms of theory, experiments, and logical conclusions and to create instead a field of innocence where the animal could become the teacher.

Here we were, a group of eight women and two men, willing to experience this communication process and see what would result. Pioneers, experimenters, researchers. I felt a great warmth for these new friends who so trustingly entered an environment that was unfamiliar to them.

THE HAWAIIAN SPINNER DOLPHINS

There in the water were the dolphins ! We saw the three-toned color pattern of the Spinner Dolphins, smaller than Bottlenose, approximately five to six feet in length, fulfilling their part by coming to meet us. I had heard rumors that Spinner Dolphins were shy and avoided swimmers. Another myth put to rest.

We had motored slowly through the waters during the past few days. Daily they came to ride our bow waves. Stopping the boat, we waited quietly, watching their amazing flying feats in and above the water, enjoying the show, feeling love and appreciation for their synchronized movements and speedy, weaving behavior just below the surface of the clear Hawaiian waters. We felt privileged as we experienced the contentment that floods your soul when you know beauty and order prevail in the universe.

We began to feel the desire to join them... as a child who wants to try what other children in the schoolyard are doing. We were filled with visions of ourselves as agile ocean-swimmers, able to move effortlessly through the unresisting water, flying and diving into the blue sky or the depths of the welcoming ocean. We knew we could do it. It was more than a thought... it was a deep inner knowing.

Still mindful of our entrance into the dolphins' environment, we proceeded slowly, one at a time, no hurry, no sense of limited time. Time would wait for us. The dolphins wanted to meet us and they would be there when we entered the water. These thoughts entered our minds, and we were thoughtful and helpful of each other... offering assistance with snorkels, masks and fins. Some people quietly lowered themselves into the cool water, others waited and watched attentively.

Would the dolphins leave? We knew their sonar could scan our bodies at distances exceeding five miles in the ocean. The water suddenly became still. Not a dolphin to be seen as three swimmers glided effortlessly away from the aft of the boat. No splashing. The swimmers knew the 'dolphin swim.' Hands quietly at their sides or clasped behind their back, legs kicking slowly with deep strokes, heads in the water breathing through the snorkel tube. They made very little wake.

After a breathless moment, someone aboard the boat silently pointed to a cresting wave one hundred feet away. The transparent wave was filled with sleek bodies of dolphin pods, glistening in the morning sunshine. Then as if by magic, fins began to appear around the boat, slicing the water in all directions, creating a maze of motion and patterns. The ocean was suddenly alive with activity, and it was focused around us. Wherever we looked, we saw dolphins. Jumping, zooming, swimming sideways past us, gazing intently at us and coming back to look again. There was no mistaking the communication. They were there to see us, to investigate us, to play with us, to invite us into their world. Their invitation was clear and exuberant. We would not resist their call to play and learn from them. Happily, respectfully, we joined them in the water. Our human pod temporarily disbursed for personal and individual encounters with the groups of dolphins that swirled around us.

COMMUNICATING WITH OCEAN DOLPHINS

Looking through our face masks down into the sun-speckled particles of light that danced in the water, we watched the Spinner Dolphins rub their bellies on the soft sand below. Swimming side by side, touching each other, suddenly rocketing, spiraling, gently to the surface near us, breaking the water, flying in the air and taking a breath in unison with our own spouting of water from our snorkels. Together, we dived, side by side, human and dolphin, graceful in the buoyant water, heading down into the deep, feeling the pop in our ears as the air pressure equalized itself in our air cavities. Deeper still and then finally arching upward again moving our fins in unison with their flukes, to break the surface together and spout and inhale. Timelessness, as we watched, mimicked and participated in their playtime.

Two dolphins are gliding directly towards me on the water's surface. I am provided another view of them as they approach, eyeing me, head on. I remain in quiet flotation. What will they do? Right in front of me now, they effortlessly separate, one to each side, and make a full circle returning to swim side by side, with me in the middle. Feeling them next to me, enclosed in their dyadic field, being one of them, being a dolphin if only for a moment. Then they are diving, and I am diving with them, trailing behind; they seem to wait for me. And then with a simple flick of their flukes, they disappear in the distant expanses of blue.

Now I notice dolphins above me. Some Bottlenose dolphins have arrived. One of them has a sucker fish attached to his side, which waves and trails in the water in a benign way. They are very interested in what we are doing, and swim directly to me, facing me eye to eye. Their smiling wide-eyed look is so intent and curious, that I laugh spontaneously at them. They appear so child-like and yet so wise.

Surfacing, I look around to see what other group members are doing. Everywhere I look, I see indistinct backs of heads bobbing in the water with iridescent snorkel tubes protruding from them, surrounded by fins and sleek dark dolphins in all arrays of positions and movement. Each person focused on the deep blue water below them, each having their own unique experience of interaction with these free-swimming dolphins. Experiences we will share later when we meet in circle at our temporary mutual home on land.

Each beautiful sunshiny day continued, as the love among ourselves and the dolphins grew.

On our last day out to sea, a feeling of unvoiced sadness permeated our group. We knew this magical voyage was nearly over, and thoughts of home and details of travel were on our minds.

None of this however, overshadowed the enthusiasm of each person when the dolphins majestically swam out to meet us again. With unabashed love and appreciation we greeted them joyfully. After a leisure hour of swimming with them in the water, it was time to return to shore, and to bring to an end this group experience.

A BOTTLENOSE BIRTH

We had one more wonderful surprise in store for us. As we turned our catamaran homeward, we came upon a pod of seven Bottlenose dolphins. Elders, it appeared from their extensive scars and huge size, probably weighing 400 pounds or more. They immediately changed direction and began riding our bow waves. We continued on our way, glad to have their company as they twisted and wove back and forth between the hulls of our catamaran. We sat so close to them that we pulled our legs up out of the water to avoid accidently bumping them with our feet.

One of the dolphins had a remora attached to it, and we watched with fascination as this sucker fish flapped from side to side in the bow waves. The dolphins slowed and fell back into the deep under the boat, while another group of their pod took their places at the bow of our boat.

Then we saw it ! The three of us riding the bow of the boat noticed another protuberance coming from a twisting and weaving dolphin. Thinking it another remora, we looked with interest. Then we looked again. It was not a remora. Coming out of the underside of this dolphin was a tiny replica of a full sized dolphin. It was revealing itself tail first, and as we watched, more and more of it's perfect body became visible. It was a baby dolphin, and right before our incredulous eyes, as its mother swam and rode the waves, the baby was being born !

At that moment we lost any reserve we may still have had, and screaming at the top of our lungs, we told everyone else, "Its a baby ! She's having a baby !" We watched wide-eyed as the dolphin baby turned slowly out of the mother's womb, seeing its veins and delicate skin right beneath our eyes as the mother kept pace with the front of our boat ! Before the birth completed, the mother slowed and dropped into the depths below, leaving us to nearly fall overboard in our efforts to follow her disappearing form.

What a wonderful gift. Our week with the dolphins had come to an end, but we knew it was actually a beginning. All of us had been changed by the interactions. We had entered the ocean world, releasing the constraints of gravity. We had listened to its sounds, floated in its currents, and absorbed its startling blue colors. We met with the graceful residents of this magical place, and we were welcomed into their home. We experienced how this peaceful environment can foster harmony and playfulness among those who open their senses and their sensitivity to its beauty, light and movement. Nothing in our lives would be the same. We had been touched by the dolphins and their world.

It had been a demonstration of learning through love and play. We learned about being a pod, about cooperation and the joy of living. We appreciated simplicity and a feeling of being safe in the world. We were expressing our creativity through art, dance, spiritual awareness, and pro-posals of joint humanitarian projects. We had a desire to remain together, and to work together. Our self-esteem was enhanced by feelings of unconditional love, and we recognized our Oneness with nature, animals, all people and the ocean.

In a few weeks we would learn of healings that had occurred. Of life changes, new careers, mended relationships, and a sudden connection with other people who had also had dolphin encounters. New worlds, dreams and hopes were ignited. And somehow each person had become a catalyst for dolphin love.

Experiencing the dolphins expanded empathic communications this time, I understood there is a way to create this same process on the land as in the ocean, and that it can be experienced among people using the conduit of air as well as water.

They made me aware of my own capabilities in empathic communica-tions. An ability that can be used whether dolphins are present or not.

For their teachings, I am eternally grateful.

Immersing in golden light and focusing our intentions
for the well-being of our global and personal bodies,
we form a group mind that connects energetically
to other experiences of evolving creation.
Moving beyond our perceptions, we span the awareness
to exalted, encoded wave lengths...
to the wisdom of the spheres.
As matter and consciousness pulsate together,
we express our emerging potentials,
journeying into another reality of
the universe and its wonders.

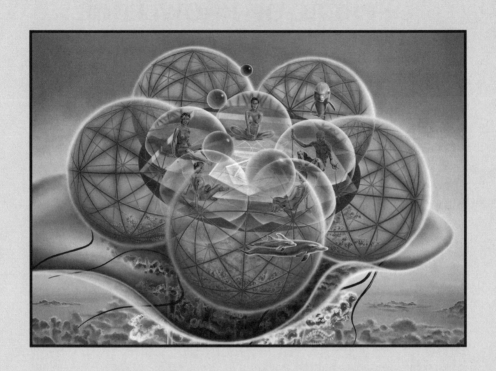

7

SPHERE OF KNOWLEDGE

I began to experience this expansive method of communication with nature and with other people when Jean-Luc and I decided to end our travels temporarily and live by the ocean in Hawaii. It was the first time in many years we experienced the luxury of knowing we did not need to check out of a hotel by 11:00 AM. We had enjoyed our travels, and now we were in total bliss in our new home !

Looking out at 5000 miles of ocean all day, we breathe deeply. We also enjoy the profusion of fresh Hawaiian fruits and vegetables. Eating the most healthy foods, washing everything thoroughly, taking optimal care of our bodies, exercising, and spending hours in nature. It continues to be a very healthy life, and very natural. Swimming every day, as many times as we wish. We are living our dream, as Jean-Luc paints a new series of artwork*, and I write and answer letters.

THE OCEAN IS MY TEACHER

On a few occasions after swimming far from land and floating dreamily on the startling blue waters, I began to have some amazing experiences. A thought I had never had before, would enter my mind, followed by a flood

---

*Art available as colorful laminated notecards from the Dolphin Connection (Appendix).

of information regarding that thought.

For example, I felt myself comingling with particles of the water, feeling as though the water were flowing in me and through me, as though my body had become a fluid substance. I let myself remain in that easy dream state.

I then began to understand how the molecules of water and air interact with each other and with our physical forms that have the same composition. I 'saw' how thought forms are carried by the oxygen in the water. How other forms in the water have their essences, their vibrating physical matter, moving into the streams of liquid, and connecting with other conscious forms there. I understood how messages can be conveyed on this air-water conduit, and that this is a method of receiving the awareness of other life forms.

I experienced a vision of what appeared to be water sprites or nature spirits in the ocean. They were an expression of thoughtforms and feelings that originated within the ocean. These patterns had flowing shapes that were sometimes visible to the human eye.

WAVES AND PARTICLES

On subsequent occurrences of this blending-experience in the ocean during my solitary swims, I understood how molecules of matter and energy can form and reform, can become solid or liquid, waves or particles.

The influence of our thoughts, was one explanation for these changing characteristics.

Thoughtforms that transformed matter and energy were not individual thoughts, but the combined thought waves of many people and patterns that had merged to become one strength.

I understood there are no 'accidents of nature.' Everything we consider solid and real has evolved from the consciousness of each tiny atom of its energy, and is held in place by the continuing thoughtforms of that energy.

This meant that these conscious atoms could change the Earth as we know it... to recreate it, reform it, to change its structure or destruct it, to rearrange itself through an energy re-organization or a transformation. (Transformation in this example, meaning a transfer of information.)

This information merged beyond words with my awareness. It was exciting to me, because I understood that if energy is consciously creating the universe, we can direct that energy-awareness to create a universe that is healthy and peaceful !

It also brought home to me very dramatically the fact that our bodies, our minds, and our pulsating Earth are all a part of this on-going decision that holds the Earth together. We have a responsibility (a response ability) to participate in this constant decision-making process with integrity and universal awareness.

OUR CRYSTALLINE BODIES

This system of communication was experienced in the water, but I soon began to receive these large quantities of information when I was quiet, alone, sitting on the beach or in my living room. I experienced this communication as an energy field that surrounded me like a 'Bubble' or 'Sphere,' within which, I was totally immersed in the expansive data waves.

This was not an experience of channeling or meditation. The energy field appeared as an expansion of my own aura. It originated from my body's bioelectric, crystalline system, and was triggered by a harmony with nature and a sense of health and well-being. This reminded me of the state of mind that is experienced in dolphin contacts. Perhaps this harmonic wavelength activates a chemical reaction in my DNA or cell structures that creates this electric field. It is as though multiple brain synapses are all firing at once, but not merely in my brain. The data-receptors in my entire body are activated.

THE ANSWERS ARE WITHIN

As I continued to relax into this mind expansion, I began to understand more and more through my own processes, the method of communication that the dolphins were using and trying to communicate to humans who hoped to break the barriers in interspecies communication.

It is a method that by-passes words and uses holographic imagery, tones, and feelings to convey huge quantities of knowledge in a brief time. In some way it stimulates a knowledge-bank that already exists within the cell structure of humans. Within the very fiber of vibrating physical matter, in humans and in cetaceans, and probably in all life forms.

The quality of its expression may be dependent on the being's level of evolutionary awareness. That is, the extent of communication is limited only by the individual's natural or conscious ability to connect their cellular vibration to the others, or to nature, and to guide the communication towards specific subject matters or sensations. It requires a two-way participation between the sender and the receiver, i.e., people who do not want this communication will not perceive it.

When people are in a receptive state of mind, and the feelings of open hearted love, gratitude or inspiration prevail, 'telempathy' is possible.

The wisdom that is transmitted affects both the subtle and the physical bodies... reminding us that spirit and body are not separate. Our bodies exist within our consciousness. They are a high frequency expression of consciousness, a physical manifestation of our spiritual energy. This holographic communication teaches all of our mind and body simultaneously.

EXPANDED COMMUNICATION

When I began this process with the dolphins and whales, I felt their love for the planet. It was so deeply experienced that I was changed by the communication. I became a protector of the planet and its inhabitants. The knowledge infused my mind and body, and led to a change in my lifestyle. It was not merely an input of new data, it was a change of mental attitude and belief systems, accompanied by physical changes in my body; which became apparent over time.

This is the new level of communication I believe is available to everyone. It exists around us. It is accessed through feelings. It contacts the mind in all of the body's cells, it engages the intellect, it includes holographic imagery, it reveals a total piece of information (all inclusive), it becomes a permanent memory within the cell structure. It does not need to be recorded linearly or verbalized, it is absorbed into the body, and it is accessible when needed. This expansive new form of communication has always been available. Now we can tap into it as we live our lives within the divine flow of harmony. It is a process that can be stimulated by a particular frequency, tone or feeling,

"Our Minds are part of a Universal Mind, uncontained in any brain or any body. We can access this Mind when we set aside our physical attachments and let our spirit roam free. In this freedom, we visit many dimensions and spaces in realms that vibrate compatibly with our own frequency. We are learners and teachers in the spiritual realms. We understand why we have chosen a physical incarnation and how it is helping us to purify our frequencies to permit travel into the higher patterns of Radiant Light."

which resonates compatibly with the intelligence in our cells. Its wisdom permeates our physical/energy matter.

THE WAVES IN OUR ATMOSPHERE

The cetaceans, living a simple lifestyle in the receptively enhanced currents of water, are not limited by belief systems and enculturation that denies feelings and tones, as a practical method of communication. In their watery environment, they feel and experience vibrational patterns that carry information to their sensory systems, to their entire mind in their body.

We may not live in the water, but we can use the conduit of air, to have the same experiences on land.

For example, I have seen the vision of Earth with the electronic impulses of our mass communication systems surrounding it. It looks like a globe with overlapping lines of communication cables encircling it. We are connected to that vast system through the electro-impulses of our biochemical body. The extensive network of computers, facsimile machines, satellite hook-ups and international electronic connections, transmit waves into our atmosphere that affect our own magnetic fields. These energy impulses are a growing part of our Earth's bio-feedback to us.

There has been concern that these electric and magnetic fields generated by these overhead cables pose a threat to human health causing everything from learning disorders to cancer.

However, the opposite can be true. While participating in this electronic communication network, people can transmit positive thoughts and ideas along them. These vast waves of communication serve as an electronic system to transmit harmonic and healing vibrations to the planet.

As we meditate and monitor our thinking to emit positive thoughtforms or loving energy fields, we are assisted by the power lines which amplify and propel our thoughts.

EVERYTHING IS MOVING FASTER

These networks-of-impulses are carrying information that interacts with our feeling or vibrational bodies. No wonder everything seems to be moving faster these days ! A deluge of information is impacting our minds and bodies in every moment.

We do not need to feel overwhelmed by it, if we realize we can effectively utilize it.

The dolphins *focus* their sending and receiving energy-waves with the use of their sonar sensors.* Humans can do this too. For example, in this chapter I mention waves and particles in regard to the evolution of the Earth as a process of evolving thoughtforms... everything that we know has evolved from the consciousness of each tiny atom of energy, and is held in place by the continuing thoughtforms of that energy.

We are the ones who are participating in the transmission of those thoughtforms. We send out the thoughtforms that create our own world. Since we are the ones involved in this creative process, we can decide to change the thoughts we are emitting, or to increase the positive thoughts and good intentions and bring about a change in the physical world.

We can access this knowledge, and realize this is just a beginning for humankind. Once we understand that patterns of information exist within all matter, within our Earth, and in our atmosphere; we realize these thoughtforms are also a part of the physical matter that comprises our genetic make-up, our bodies and its consciousness. Rather than being a 'channel' of energy, we connect to the entire communication network that stems from our own physical-matter body. We are the hub or nucleus of this expansive communication system. We take responsibility for the in-flow and out-flow.

CHANGES IN OUR CELLS

Biologists have studied our cell structure and the nucleic acid that is called DNA. They have found that cells reproduce themselves with regularity (Appendix). Our human form is re-created annually by continually producing

---

Whales Dolphins and Porpoises, Richard Harrison, Michael Bryden, consulting editors; Facts on File Inc., New York, 1988, pg.130.

new cells. In most areas the new cells are replications of the old, but when we change the vibrational frequency of our physical matter, we are changing the matter that composes our cells.

Entering the sphere of knowledge or the unified pool of deep inner harmony, we realize we can change our vibrational frequency to one that can communicate with dolphins, to one that can generate healthy cells in our body, and to one that can expand into dimensions of communication that exist in the ethers all around us. For example, we can communicate with all the light frequencies beyond our present sight and hearing, and we can access communication networks that extend beyond the Earth.

Practising changing our own frequency-patterns into wave lengths of love and harmony, helps us to fine tune ourselves to a particular wave length other than our current one. By so doing, we eventually change the very cells of our bodies. For most of us it is a new way of communicating, and yet it is readily accessible. Some of our meditations change our wave lengths in similar ways.

GROUP MEDITATION

During the past five years, Jean-Luc and I have travelled with our Dolphin Connection presentation, beginning every program with a meditation.

The positive effects of meditation are well documented. Meditation stimulates a relaxed, receptive state of mind that releases stress and physical tension, allowing people to enjoy a period of quietness in their mind and body. By beginning our Dolphin Connection show with a meditation, the audience can more fully experience and absorb our 'right brain' presentation of colors, tones and sacred architecture moving before them in our audio-visual screening.

However, group meditation accomplishes much more than that. In hotels, theaters and church halls, we have joined with groups of people to create certain healing vibrations and etheric geometric forms, to interact with our energy fields and stimulate, harmonize, and anchor positive frequencies. They move from our own spiraling circle, into our planet and beyond... connecting to the impulses, grids, and triangulations that exist in the expansive universal world.

These meditations remind us that all things are possible when we combine our loving intentions for the health and well being of our global and personal bodies. We create a group mind that energetically connects to all of the loving vibrations of the Universe. Like attracts like !

This reminds me of a wonderful story that occurred during Summer Solstice in Hawaii. It is a story of the power of love and the positive energy of transmuted fear.

FOR THOSE WHO FEAR THE WATER

There are some people who feel as much at home in the water as they do walking across a field of tall grass. This section is not for you ! This is for those people who are attracted to the water, love to go to the beach, want to sail on boats, but they have an irrational, nameless and sometimes outright embarrassing fear of being in the water. While travelling to different locations, I have met an unusually high percentage of those people. They all seem to love dolphins. Perhaps I am attracting them. Like attracts like, is the scientific and metaphysical explanation !

I wouldn't begin to try and unravel the karmic reasons for these reactions to the ocean, but I will acknowledge their reality for many people. In the light of creating my own reality, I will no longer label myself as one of those people. But... I can remember when... !

Recently, I invited a group of people to swim with me and the dolphins in the coastal waters of Hawaii. One of the participants of this Dolphin Ocean Swim was a man, age 45, who fit the description above in his fear of the water. Confiding that he had this fear, Sam decided to attend the week-long seminar anyway. He came with great trepidation. He also came with hundreds of dollars worth of gear to keep him afloat, and as an incentive to himself to enter the water. He had wonderful determination.

On the first day of our Dolphin Ocean Swim, my adventurous friend began to prepare his gear in readiness for the arrival of dolphins. Our dolphin friends did not disappoint us. In a short time the rest of the people were donning their snorkels and fins for a cooling dip and dolphin swim. Eventually, Sam was ready, hardly recognizable in his iridescent hat, wet suit, buoyancy compensator, face mask, booties, and fins. As the boat captain and I waited (hopefully unobtrusively), Sam completed adjusting his zippers and straps, and with sweat pouring from his brow looked up at us question-ingly.

Ready? Ready. The boat had no ladder, and he was uncertain about how to get to the water. After detailed instructions about climbing into the ocean from the end of the Boston Whaler, Sam was willing to try it. He had his flippers on so that complicated the task. Finally three of us cooperated in helping him into the water. It was a clear and calm day. The ocean was warm and relatively gentle. Sam, however, would not release his grip on the top side of the boat. Only the bottom half of his body was submerged. The rest clung desperately to the side of the boat while his knuckles turned white from the strain. Now I am describing this in a comical way but I know it is not funny for those who understand very well what Sam was feeling. It wasn't funny for Sam either. The boat captain and I felt immeasurable love for him and his stalwart courage.

We also had compassion for this fear that held him in agony clinging to the rocking boat. We placed a life preserver in the water next to him, suggesting he hold on to that instead. With a great show of trust in us and a deep realization that it was 'now or never,' he splashed out one arm to grab the life preserver, hesitated as it temporarily submerged from his weight, and then released his other hand from its painful grip on the boat's edge and held tightly to the preserver.

Immediately the life preserver began drifting away from the side of the boat. A look of panic crossed Sam's face. His fear made breathing difficult. Another swimmer joined him, while Sam removed his snorkel, an unnec-essary obstruction since his head was above water.

With another swimmer close by, he looked up at me on the boat and weakly returned my okay signal with a smile. He was afloat and he could breathe. For now that was enough.

Sam didn't stay very long in the water that day. He was exhausted. But the next day he went in again. Staying close to the boat, on our second day at sea, the dolphins came to him. As they swam around him and dove down, he learned to put his face in the water to see them. He forgot his fear, and began to breathe easily through the snorkel... grateful for this gear that allowed him to see the beauty of the agile dolphins as they glided and circled beneath him. None of us knew the dolphins were there by the boat, as we all swam into the ocean with another pod.

Sam was different after that. When we returned to our living accommodations on land that afternoon, he had a wonderful story to tell about his special pod of dolphins that looked at him and invited him to play and demonstrated all their techniques !

By the third day, Sam was swimming with ease. He was an inspiration to all of us, and a constant reminder to me of how to overcome fear: determination, common sense, help from friends and the love of the dolphins !

On the Dolphin Ocean Swim expeditions no one is required to swim in the ocean. Each participant has the choice, but we do encourage people to join us on the boats and immerse themselves into the 'dolphin experience' as fully as possible. This is because the focus of these gatherings is to create a 'group bond' or energy field that increases with each day we are together, and teaches us to creatively use our potentials towards earth healing and humanitarian purposes.

CO-CREATING OUR WORLD

As we immerse ourselves in these powerful group energies, we understand the concept of co-creating our world. The energy force is amplified by the combined merging of our crystalline structures. As we send healing rays into the environment, we are simultaneously receiving the healing ourselves. We are not separate from the consciousness that pulsates in our physical matter, and we are not separate from the consciousness that we send out. We are creating a reality, at the same time we are participating in it.

In fact, we are doing this during every moment of our lives on this physical plane. The collective consciousness of all of Earth's inhabitants creates our physical reality and holds the Earth together in form. When we, as a group, participate in the same process, but decide consciously to choose a healing frequency to send out, perhaps using crystals, colors, nature, spiritual guides, circles, spirals, triangles, domes, and other advanced universal patterns to amplify our own, we easily radiate harmonic frequencies from our group field into the vibrating thoughts on and around the planet. We see the world in its perfection, and it becomes what we 'see.'

Understanding that we change our vibrational frequency through our feelings, we begin to take responsibility for the feelings and thoughts we emit.

Remembering that our thoughts and feelings lead to the creation of physical matter, and to the re-creation of our cells, we can heal our bodies if we so choose; in the same way that we use our transmissions, consciously or unconsciously, to create our world.

UNIVERSAL QUESTIONS AND ANSWERS

In addition to learning how to access at will, feelings of love and harmony; I have entered this expansive communication sphere in other ways.

In the water with the cetaceans, I am feeling great joy and happiness. These feelings supersede everything else and provide the access route to the advanced communication network. But when I am relaxing in my outdoor canvas chair, the experience of the Sphere of Knowledge is often preceded by feelings of appreciation and gratitude, especially for the beauty of nature.

Another stimulus can be a thought that relates to my global/universal interests. It can be stimulated by reading an inspirational book, or by a sudden understanding that serves to bridge seemingly unrelated pieces of information that I have previously received. This small node of information fires the mind with new possibilities, thoughts, feelings and applications.

Have you ever been in a group where people are sharing experiences or asking questions of a channel? Many of the questions revolve around self-help and problem solving. Then all at once someone asks a profound and spiritually significant question that applies to the spiritual growth of everyone there.

A change occurs. You can feel the difference in the room. Now the group has moved into a higher frequency. The information coming back or filling the room is of a more advanced level.

This is how we can elevate ourselves into accelerated energies of universal harmony, through profound and loving thoughts. We can do it in a group and we can do it in our own lives. Since universal love is one of my favorite subjects, I have written more about this in the following chapters.

In the next chapter, I will give you an example of some additional information I received while experiencing the Sphere of Information. Each Sphere that encompasses me, seems to contain very specific themes.

8

THOUGHTFORMS AND RESPONSE ABILITY

etween July and October, 1988, I received information from the Sphere of Knowledge experiences that included topics such as Energy Re-channeling, Beyond Physical Matter, Planetary Enlightenment, DNA and Transformation. Portions of these topics are included in this book as they relate to the growing awareness of humanity's role in group consciousness.

OUR EMOTIONS AND FEELINGS —
NEUROPEPTIDES IN THE BODY

Neuropeptides are chemical substances made and released by brain cells and certain other cells in the body. Neuropeptides float through all the body fluids and are attracted to specific Receptors in the body. Neuropeptides and the Receptors grow directly off of the DNA. They create an information network or a communication system in the body. The Neuropeptides are molecules that send messages all over the body. They are the components that 'talk.' The Receptors are the components that 'hear.' The Receptor sites throughout the body receive the Neuropeptides and a change occurs in the physical body, in the organs and cellular structures of the body.

Biochemists, in their study of physiology, have recently completed experiments that indicate our neuropeptides are related to our feelings or emotions, and that our feelings can be the determining factor in the health or deterioration of our body's organs.

For example, their research indicates that a person could be completely sated with water and not thirsty at all; but if their feeling of thirst is activated by artificially stimulating their thirst-neuropeptide, that neuropeptide will travel through the body to the kidney and the kidney, though filled with liquid, will begin to conserve water as if thirst actually existed. That means that the feeling leads to a physiological change or response in the organs.

As metaphysicians, we have always known that our feelings affect our bodies, but it is interesting to understand the process as described by the biologists and scientists. (Appendix)

Our emotions are expressed through neuropeptides. As they float through the body and move to specific 'landing sites,' they affect the health (or disease) of our body... of our organs, according to what those feelings are.

ENERGY RE-CHANNELING

I am affecting the health of my body by choosing the feelings or emotions that will occupy and influence it. I am doing this by becoming aware of what I am feeling, taking a moment to listen to my body, or experience it, deciding rationally if the emotion or feeling is health-promoting for me, and then choosing to allow it to remain or choosing to change what I am feeling. I find this can be done.

Being a psychologist, I am aware of the folly of denying feelings and blocking emotions. I am careful not to do that. If I need to cry, I cry. If I need to shout, I shout. If I want to laugh, I laugh, and so on. What I will no longer do is to run the negative thoughts or feelings over and over again in my mind. I am learning to release it quickly. If the feelings are difficult to simply release, as they often seem to be, I will make a conscious decision to *re-channel* the energy through one means or another.

One method of re-channeling energy is accomplished through physical action. This requires an exercise or activity in which I exert so much effort and concentration that there is no excess energy available for disease-promoting thoughts or feelings to permeate the body. As a novice swimmer, speed-swimming in the ocean is one example of a means of redirecting my energy. Instead of spending energy on negative thoughts, I channel my energy into something useful.

AWARENESS EXPANSION

Another method of energy re-channeling and re-labeling that can be very effective is what I have called, 'Awareness Expansion.' This is a process in which I expand my understandings of a situation to a Universal level.

That is, I review my problem or unhealthy emotion from a universal point of view. How would this predicament or occurrence appear to an evolved person from another solar system? How does this turmoil in my life affect the universe? Imagining a universal beings eye-view of our emotional upheavals can be quite awesome. Perhaps they wonder why we permit some of our life experiences to create disease and damage in our physical and magnetic bodies. If our daily experiences are understood as opportunities for evolvement along our spiritual path, then why do we, humans, act as if these experiences are devastating and even life-threatening? For example, there was a time when I owned a condominium which I decided to rent while I travelled to be with the dolphins. I had constant problems with this rental unit, from repair bills to bounced rental checks. I was a landlady who was unavailable.

Many nights I laid awake worrying about being able to meet my mortgage payments. Trying to sell the property did not work either. The tenant managed to deter all possible buyers by telling them the real and imagined problems of the dwelling. I seemed doomed to endure this annoying block to total freedom.

Finally, in exasperation I was ready to give the property away just to remove the stress.

Just in time, I began to understand the concept of 'Awareness Expansion.' I realized this situation was providing a useful learning process for me and if I gave the condo away to rid myself of the problem, it would return to me in another form. My higher self seemed determined to guide me through this spiritual lesson !

Now, what was the lesson? I had the feeling that giving the property away was not the lesson I needed to learn.

STRESS TO HARMONY

Instead, I needed to effectively work out a solution, to take it in hand and solve it. Approaching my tenant and my real estate agent from a place of loving cooperation and releasing fears of not being able to pay the mortgage, I talked to my tenant openly about my reasons for selling the condo. I agreed to her request to remain for two more months in the condominium. After two months she moved out as agreed, I cleaned the condo, contacted the agent and sold it.

It seems simple, but for some reason I held on to this problem for years. Perhaps I had an unconscious resistance to selling it, due to unresolved security fears. I believed I was doing everything possible to correct the situation, but I felt angry about it until I changed my perception and began to accept it as a valuable learning tool I was providing for myself. Instead of being angry about it, I showered it with love and light.

Our attitude about our perceived difficulties is key to our bodily reactions. Can we move through these lessons of life with determination, curiosity and even gratitude, strengthening our ability to maintain a harmonic presence no matter what befalls us? I believe we can do this. We can live in the world like the Saints and Masters who live in the world, but are not of the world. Living here, remembering who we are as spiritual beings and not getting lost in emotional and physical problems of the materialistic, reactionary world. Can we do it?

I think we can. During an immersion in a 'Bubble of Information,' I understood that so many aware people have already removed themselves from the life styles and incentives of the collective consciousness or the sleeping masses. We have remembered our greater purposes or we are seeking them. We know what we don't want and are open to guidance through love for what we do want.

When we examine the events in our lives in relation to our aeons of lifetimes as spiritual beings, we can understand that what appear to be mammoth problems are merely a drop in the time-space of our evolving souls ! They are important as tools, as learning devices; but in perspective, they are very insignificant.

When I experience this Awareness Expansion in relation to my current and reoccurring lessons here, my awareness grows and my understanding allows me to be at peace with many potentially difficult situations.

EXAMINING HABITS

There are many habits we have each developed and unthinkingly slip into whenever we have a problem or a situation that requires our attention. In most cases we are so programed by these habits, that we rarely open ourselves to new possibilities. Could it be that some of our reactions and feelings are nothing more than pre-programed responses?

When we think someone has insulted us, we may feel anger or hurt. The feeling seems to arise automatically. Perhaps it relates to experiences from our childhood. We may believe we are the helpless victims of these angry or hurt feelings, or that we have a 'right' to feel this way. Yet I know some people who react to this same type of insult situation with compassion for the perpetrator. They do not experience anger or hurt. This would indicate that some feelings we assume are universal, automatic, and correct, are not that at all.

Our feelings are a force of energy within us. Whether we experience happiness, anger, sadness or pain, it is all an experience of energy that is being utilized in a way that we can feel it and identify it.

My learnings in the Sphere of Knowledge continued... showing me that everything is energy. It is not static, it does not disappear, it changes and rearranges itself. We can work with energy. It can be focused, expanded, transformed, diffused, mutated, constricted, increased and transcended.

Over periods of time, people have assigned labels to certain qualities of energy that are experienced in the physical body. These are called feelings and through a collective cultural agreement (the reality consensus), types of energy are labeled as specific feelings and then categorized to be good or bad. Our belief systems about the positive or negative aspects of life then permit these feelings to lead to behaviors that are congruent with our beliefs.

When a loved one has been unkind to us, we feel a flow of energy that we label, and then react to, by being angry, tense or withdrawn. Our behaviors and feelings send signals into our body via neuropeptides, which affect our internal organs. If we are experiencing stressful feelings and behaviors, our organs can atrophy due to constricted breathing, loss of body elasticity, and the unnatural vibratory rate of the energy we are running or producing. It is unnatural because it is at variance with nature, as expressed in the harmonic pulsations of our cellular DNA patterns and in the resonant frequency of approximately 7.5 cycles per second (Appendix). It is healthful to remedy this stressful energy flow as soon as possible.

One way to do this is to engage in an activity or thought process that creates happiness. Think of something wonderful that's coming up in the days ahead, plan something wonderful, get a massage, buy some new clothes, spend a day doing what YOU want to do. Whatever it takes, do it immediately to very purposefully change your debilitating feelings to ones of peace and power. When we succumb to feelings that reflect powerlessness, we are harming our physical and subtle bodies.

Another re-direction choice changes the vibratory rate of the energy we are experiencing. In the 1950s Dr. John Lilly, found that dolphins would change the energy they were experiencing by shaking all over and dispersing negative stimulation, rather than expressing it as aggressive behavior among themselves.

As many people have learned, meditation is a very effective tool for changing our vibratory rate. When we move into a deep state of meditation, we are in harmony with the natural pulse of our body. We are at peace, and the body receives the benefit.

At this point in our spiritual awareness, it is important that we WILL ourselves to do these things. To recognize our habits and alter them when they are harmful for our spirit and body. Eventually, we will automatically redirect the energy. It will be a natural outgrowth of living happy, healthy lives. This is what we are aiming for. The state of harmony that reflects our natural, loving selves and in which the divine force flows.

AMAZING THINGS HAPPEN

When we are in harmony, we no longer respond to situations with negativity, but with understanding, compassion, and even joy. We have power and control over our personal world in the same way that I believe the dolphins and whales do. They choose every breath they breathe and they choose to live in love. It is also their natural response to the world of joy in which they live.

I have developed a simple technique that works well when I am faced with a potentially stressful situation. I ask myself the question: "What is the most loving thing I can do right now?"

Proceeding according to the answer to that question has always brought the most satisfying results. In addition, the tension in my body is immediately alleviated when I begin to examine the problem from that point of view. I truly am a loving person, and approaching challenges in life from that mind-frame allows me to express who I am. The answer may not always be in keeping with what society tells you to do, or even what you've done before, but it will be the most nurturing answer, and the consequences may surprise and please you. Amazing things begin to happen !

The interesting effects of the journey into our innate harmonic frequencies, known as Love, is that we then resonate with the Creative Elements of the world. The Creative Energy or Element is a mammoth, self-sufficient system in which everything moves in cycles and is overlapping and inter-reactive. Within this system, all of the energy extensions support each other with manifestations that fulfill the vibrating collective desires or thoughtforms of the individual parts. For example, every flower receives water when it is thirsty, and every human receives food, knowledge or money, etc. when they *desire* it. It is a natural energy flow that matches the energy of desire or intent with the energy that creates matter.

You may think you are not experiencing this yet. Most likely you are, but your thoughts and feelings may be different than what you would choose them to be. If our thoughtforms are negative and self-defeating, our life reflects those thoughts. When our higher purposes cannot align with our negative or fearful thoughts, our energy does not flow freely. We cannot manifest our heart's desire, if our doubts, fears and low self-esteem over rule our hopes and dreams.

FROM THOUGHTS TO MATTER

We can have every good and perfect thing we want in life when our energy flows freely into the creative system that holds this planet together.

As I understood so clearly while experiencing the Sphere of Knowledge, this natural process in which we are the creators and recreators of the planet through our vibrating thoughtforms and feelings, is very much like the process of the recreation of cells in our body. In the same way that we interact with and manifest the physical matter on our planet; so do we do likewise with our bodies. We have a choice about what we will create. As we recognize our ability to control our thoughts and produce health in the world, returning it to a body that resonates in harmony; so will we do likewise for our own physical bodies. Our uncontrolled thoughts and feelings are producing irregularities in our bodies; disease and premature death. Our uncontrolled thoughts and feelings are producing irregularities in our Earth; disease and premature death !

As we begin to examine our habits and automatic reactions, as we begin to gain control of them and our errant thoughts, as we begin to focus and choose, we will be on the threshold of a profound level of existence. Once we take 'response ability' for our thoughts and begin to understand the physics behind the power of thought among the dynamic energy systems of outer dimensionality, we will access the creative forces within us.

Within the energy field of this Creative Force or Universal Flow, we activate and escalate the genetic code within our DNA, and access untapped technological, physiological, and spiritual wisdom.

With elevated thoughts, we can access multiple dimensions, create profound living experiences on a daily basis, utilize our dormant potentials and understand that the Akashic records, or Universal knowledge, is accessed when our own cells harmoniously converge with the Creative Force.

We can transcend physical matter.

OUT OF THE BODY

As I write about transcending physical matter, I am reminded of a spontaneous out-of-body experience I had in 1975 while participating in a psychology course at California State University in Fullerton, California. As a psychologist in training, I was learning to assist people in releasing emotional and physical blocks in their bodies. I asked my associates and the course professor to facilitate a release of a block I was experiencing in my own body.

The class was meeting on the lawn of the University that day to enjoy the balmy weather. As I relaxed on the grass, surrounded by my classmates, I was gently guided by the professor to imagine myself becoming very small, and then to imagine myself as a tiny form entering into my own body to find the source of the block that I was experiencing as a painful ache in my solar plexus. This type of therapy was popular at the time, and quite effective for me because I am a visual person. I was asked to explain what the block looked like. I saw it as a wall that was impenetrable.

The professor guided me to imagine ways to penetrate the wall, and eventually I was able to do so. As I visualized myself breaking through this wall, I suddenly experienced my etheric body breaking out of my physical body. To my surprise, I was now weightless and floating about fifteen feet above my body and above the rest of the people sitting below me on the lawn.

The feelings of surprise I had were quickly replaced with a wonderful feeling of unlimitedness. This felt wonderful. I felt light and able to blend with the delicate wafts of air that circulated around me. What a glorious feeling of freedom ! There was no body weight to slow me down or move along with me. I could spin, flip, float, fly with ease. It felt very natural and I completely enjoyed the sensations. There was absolutely no fear or self-consciousness. I could see the people below me now, still focused on my quiet body, talking to me but getting no response. Meanwhile, I was joyfully floating on subtle currents of air like the tufts of a dandelion seed, or I was alternately choosing my course and floating easily in a specific direction. My mind, my personality, my understanding of who I am, was fully with me, yet I was an integral part of nature and the air we breathe.

Aside from experiencing the great peace and beauty of this feeling, I remember thinking, "This is what death is, and it is wonderful." This understanding of death was very transformative for me. I also understood that I was in complete control and that I could decide whether to return to my physical body or not. I was very tempted not to. I loved being a Light Body. It was a feeling of complete participation in all that is fascinating and beautiful.

I could hear the people below me calling to me. I could feel they were becoming concerned about my lack of response. Apparently they could not see me, floating above them.

They denied their concern by acting as though I were playing a joke on them. They began to say, "Good bye Joan. We're leaving you here. We're going to lunch."

They stood up as if to walk away. They couldn't rouse me and they weren't sure what to do.

Meanwhile, I was debating whether to return to my physical body or not. I loved the freedom of having no body. I knew I could stay this way but I understood their distress and decided to return.

The next thing I knew I was back inside my body and feeling, as if, for the first time, the sensation of solid matter beneath me. I was aware of the earth supporting my body. I dug into the grass and the rich, dark soil beneath it with my hands and heels. I experienced its richness, its aroma. I smelled the nearby pine trees, so pungent and intoxicating. I felt the penetrating rays of the warm sun on my body. I opened my eyes and was overcome by a feeling of great love for the eight people, all leaning towards me, concerned and welcoming. The sky appeared brilliant blue, the very air around me was pristine and fragrant. The gentle rustle of the wind, the colors, the world... I was an integral part of it all.

I had experienced a blending of myself with the elements. I knew without a doubt, that I was at One with nature and other people. I felt a love and connection that goes beyond words, and I was changed. I knew the reality of who I am, and I knew I was here by choice.

I was here in this body and on this planet because I wanted to be here... and I believe everyone else is here by choice also.

Many of us can share similar stories about our awakening to why we are here. Our lives on the earth plane are but shadow existences of the totality of who we are. We are connected to many energy systems that extend out from our bodies and support us in the greater universe. We can travel along these energy lines or we can send messages and receive them. We are not insular systems. We are energetically wired to multiple systems that gave birth to us eons ago. As we remember this, we begin to change our thinking. We use our dreams, music, art, and meditation to travel into other states of being. We are in contact with other distant peoples and planetarians through channeling and readings.

What we have done, is to return to a way of life that reflects our purposes for being on this planet, at this time. That is, to acknowledge and remember that we are dedicated to works that advance our spiritual evolution, and that all the activities that occupy our minds and bodies are means to that end. Contacts that some of us have with our extraterrestrial friends helps us to remember this. There is a great rejoicing in the Galaxy as more and more people on Earth awaken to their universal consciousness.

10

PYRAMIDS AND THE LIGHT STRUCTURES

his universal consciousness can be contacted as we learn to access our sphere of knowledge, our auric egg, and connect the energy field that is part of who we are, to the field of other species and life forms.

Around each flower we see, there is a field of energy that is the beauty, the aroma, the intelligence of that specific flower. In quietness and openness, we can merge our sphere of energy with that of the flower and understand its connection to the sun and the earth. We can experience this understanding and connection with a tree or a rock or a cloud. In the experience of this connection, we remember our own universal consciousness. The dolphins know this connection and they participate in its circular flow, giving and receiving love.

For many of us it is easier to relate to dolphins than to a flower. We can see they are having fun, they smile, wink their eyes and chatter to us. But our over-all patterns of energy are united in the field of consciousness that weaves all life forms together in our co-existence on this planet.

During many visualizations and writings, the patterns and weaves that unite the Earth-inhabitants have been shown to me. They are very complex sigils, which are esoteric, geometric forms. The most predominant and familiar ones are triangles and pyramids.

For those who are presently incarnated to assist in anchoring these light structures of the new way of being on Earth, I will briefly mention some of the key concepts that have been brought to light by my contacts with dolphins. This information is relayed through 'living words,' and can best be assimilated through feelings and intuition:

"The experiences of the cellular communications with the dolphins, my out-of-body incident, and the connections to the electrical impulses in our atmosphere, are related to a pattern of universal consciousness that reveals itself as architectural light structures of unending pyramids.

The path to the infinite consciousness moves through the pulsing Light Pyramids of Life, through the Divine Triads, through the Golden Mean into every structure within every possibility of creation.

The vibrating and expanding light structures of our biophysical and electrophysical bodies are unending diamonds which extend to all compatible patterns around us, from the microscopic to the universal.

Studying hydrogen atoms, we see that the pyramid is the central geometric form for all human and stellar evolution. The pyramid is a universal constant. Examining closely the hydrogen atom, we see the geometry of the star of David as the life-giving form, the six-pointed star through which we will eventually access the twelve-pointed star dimension.

The bases in our DNA molecules (Glossary) are held together by hydrogen bonding. The hydrogen atom also holds together the hydrogen matrix which uses a spin characteristic, as in a spiral, to propel our present evolutionary pattern.

The pyramid form reminds us of our connections to advanced knowledge. It is duplicated throughout the universe in physical and vibratory form, maintaining a constant configuration of precise measurements, lengths and angles which project and receive spiraling frequencies of light-energy."

THE OCEANIA PROJECT

The information regarding these human and universal forms has been of great interest to me for many years. My interest was stimulated in 1985 when Jean-Luc and I travelled to Australia where we presented our audio-visual art production to an architectural firm in Sydney. As a result of this presentation, Jean-Luc was asked to design a building as advanced in its design concepts as the beautiful Opera House enhancing Sydney Harbor. It was to be a structure destined for the Great Barrier Reef in the aqua blue waters east of Queensland.

Immediately we felt inspired by the dreams of the architects to design a structure that would be 'just beyond buildable.' So the construction company would also be inspired to greater creativity and environmental integrity in their use of various building materials.

Renting a home in beautiful Palm Beach, north of Sydney, Jean-Luc and I visualized the project as a sanctuary on the Reef, that would help to conserve and protect the dolphins and the delicate ecosystem of the coral. It would provide a means for people to enjoy the beauty of the Reef without damaging it. It could fulfill the desire to see the Reef without snorkeling or diving on it. It would be built by the coral itself through a process called electrolysis. Making it a living structure that would strengthen and add to the reef, creating an aqua botanical garden in harmony with its lagoon setting.

Jean-Luc began building the model and I began writing inspirational messages that referred to this building as a Temple and Center for transformational change. Its spiritual purposes were revealed:

"The Temple of Truth resides in the ethers since the beginning of time. It was known among the Council of Elders that humanity would be separated from their own true knowing over many eons. They would not have the eyes to see or ears to hear. Atmospheric conditions would interfere with brain waves, limiting perceptions and humans' contact with universal knowledge.

It was determined that at the appropriate time along the earth's evolutionary path, a pyramid would be constructed which would assist the human race to overcome confusion and realize the fullness of their potentials as members of the solar system.

This pyramid would be constructed over a vortex

center. It would be a full-spectrum rainbow bridge between the energies of central Earth and those of the Great Sun or Source. It would also be constructed along the current grid lines of Earth to ensure access by the Space Brotherhood. In the center of the pyramid would be the spiral of life, and within this spiral the changes would occur. Contact with the convening energy forces at the center of the spiral would bring about changes in humanity's own energy system. Confusion would be dispelled. Clarity of mind and body would allow earthlings to again access the Ancient Wisdom of Universal Knowledge and to experience space communication and travel.

This is the pyramid that moves into existence on the earth plane now. It serves as a receiver and transmitter of energies from far beyond the universe."

So, the structure was to be a pyramid of the type Jean-Luc had often envisioned and painted in his artwork. But this one was designed as a three-sided pyramid with specific geometric dimensions.

The transmissions of the cetaceans also channeled through to interact with us and the thoughtforms of this pyramid Temple:

"These are the Energies of the Dolphins and Whales. We greet you today on a Golden Ray. We connect on the transmission of this Ray and exchange our radiations of love and peace.

You are here to attract and convene with dolphin energies toward the bringing together of the multitudes of twelve. The temple of transformation of the House of Change is preparing to move onto the Earth plane now. All is being made ready and placed in order. This manifestation occurs with the collective thoughts and dreams of numerous souls who are incarnated on Earth for this reason.

The Center will involve people of many nations and will be a focalizer of peace and communication among those seeking harmony on the planet. This temple of Light will be a channel between humanity and other energy forms. As people are drawn to this sanctuary, their auric fields and cellular systems will be cleansed and balanced. This will occur through the natural radiations of ocean, earth and light. These forces will assemble with the magnetic vibrations of crystals, the earth's electromagnetic field, and the healing frequencies of lasers, colors and tones.

Dolphins will attend the gatherings and assist as guides. The physical pleasures of the water environment will include bathing pools and opportunities to swim with dolphin friends. The facility will be located on the earth's grid lines and will be a transmitter of positive, high frequency energy, assisting the Earth to maintain its rotational balance.

The usefulness of this structure on your planet is far beyond earthly imaginings. This structure has materialized during other times. Each materialization brings a variation in form and use, but its ultimate purpose is eternal.

It serves to return the human form to its blueprint pattern of unity, reuniting intellect and intuition... connecting humans to their co-creating organ, the Earth, and aligning their cellular and subtle bodies to universal vibrations."

Many more channeled messages revealed the placement and purposes of this sanctuary. After the model, paintings, and architectural blueprints were completed, Jean-Luc and I left Australia to continue sharing our Dolphin Connection presentation in the U.S.

The Oceania Project remains in the hearts and thoughtforms of those who were involved in its inception. Jean-Luc's paintings of the structure hang in the lobby of the architectural firm. Whether or not it manifests into physical form on the Great Barrier Reef remains to be seen.

The important point is that it has become a thoughtform in the ethers, where patterns of triangular Light connect us to the Universal grid system.

As Jean-Luc and I travel and share its visual and structural dimensions, the dreams of many people are activated by their inner knowledge of the significance of this Golden Triangle Pyramid.

It is a three-sided pyramid that grows from the ratios of the spiral of life, from the Fibonacci numbers and the phi calculations of 1.618 (Glossary). The angles formed in the pyramid's apex create a specific wave length of transformation (similar to what physicists call shock waves). Combined with a spiraling vortex field and a crystal capstone, it is a gateway to an accelerated frequency of Light. A person enters the pyramid and interacts with the natural or an artificially created vortex. Locating themselves on the access point to the spiral, they lay horizontally with their body at the correct angle to the apex. A linkage occurs between the pyramid's gravitational vortex and the spin orientation of the body, affecting the molecular structure of the physical form. The body releases its physical matrix and moves into another time-space zone. An electromagnetic void can be artificially created to expedite this transition. The escalating vibratory frequencies of planet Earth now support this procedure that was previously unattainable here.

I leave this pyramid thoughtform and imagery with you for your enjoyment. It will continue to enter the Earth's ethers through our dreams and memories. It is very much a part of our reality now.

As we access this coral garden
the natural healing qualities of the ocean, earth and light
will uplift us. Awakening unique
perceptions, we enter this translucent temple that
is holographically imprinted in a dimension beyond our senses,
in the patterns of triangular light that connect us to
cosmic information systems.
The Center will involve people of many worlds
and will be a focalizer of peace and communication.

THE OCEAN DOME

As a sequel to the Oceania project, I will share another vision of a high technology, dolphin communication system.

Imagine you are sitting on the beach, it's a lovely day. The sky is robin egg blue with billowy white clouds moving slowly across it. The ocean has gentle ripples and reflects another sparkling shade of blue.

All at once you think you see a huge glass building that is dome shaped, filling the horizon, floating on the ocean. You focus more intently because it is reflecting blue colors in its rounded glass sides. You are not sure if you are seeing a structure there or not. But you *can* see it. The spherical dome is either resting on the ocean or hovering just above it in the blue sky.

As you watch, you appreciate the fine design and the obvious stability of this hovering structure. You notice it is silently descending into the ocean. The dome is sinking slowly and smoothly into the blue water while the sky is reflected in its still visible ceiling.

Now it has disappeared, and you are left wondering what you saw. Then you are filled with this information:

This is a center where cetaceans and humans will interact within each others environments. You have seen our large hyper-space acceleration dome which descends on your great expanses of water, particularly the Pacific. Within the dome are ocean pools, super computers, tonal rays and laser beam technology. When we choose an appropriate landing site at a particular magnetic vortex, the pool gates open and the empty pools are filled with water. The ocean water is then prepared for human and dolphin comfort which sometimes entails a warming process. There are large and small pools. Before entering the individual-sized pool, people will enter a scanning laser field which will project his or her personal frequency pattern on a screen. This will be analyzed for energy distortions, frailties and illness. Upon entering the small pool compartments, an individual will receive a personal energy alignment and enhancement which will rejuvenate their cells for total vitality and health.

When the individual is running an unobstructed energy field and is resonating a balanced physical body, he or she may then enter the greater pools to interact with high frequency tonal rays and the multidimensional color rays. The ocean dolphins will have entered these pools and will be available to swim with people as they recall their higher frequency body waves or their original blueprint pattern that remains within their genetic coding. The dolphins use their sonar capabilities to activate the DNA substructure in the human cell system. The molecules in the human physical form have been evolving. This process is assisted by atmospheric chemicals and electromagnetic waves already in our environment. The directed energy burst from the dolphin's sonar will stimulate a chemical reaction in the cells of people. This will escalate the speed of vibration of our physical matter allowing people to connect with a sensory stimulated awareness that is more complex and expanded than our present compacted field.

It leads to activation of the memories in the DNA, which then 'reach out' to complete a cyclical pattern with the greater planetary and solar sigils (advanced geometric light shapes). Since the dolphins already live within the elevated currents of this connection to nature and creation, their presence and their wisdom will support our playful journey into expanded dimensions. What is meant by expanded dimensions is: we will realize our deep connections to the universal system, we will see more colors, hear more music, experience the beauty of our surroundings, and learn of our friendships with outerdimensional people. In this extension of our sensory potentials, people will experience a now invisible world of ideas, thoughtforms, colors, sigils, vibrating matter and spirit matter.

We will wonder why we waited so long to open ourselves to this expansive and loving world of our Creator. We will understand that we have total control of who we are, where we go, and who travels with us. We always had this choice, we just have not used it.

This is the first step towards molecular travel and transcendence.

The light of pure mind emerges
from the waves of the celestial sea.
The unseeing eyes face the unknown,
while the pentagonal sphere
hovers in the ethers,
and sustains the vibration of human
in its evolved perfection.
The crystal diamond
that is the original thoughtform of humanity is still indelible on her brow,
a pattern of clarity, a symbol of eternity.
The oceans have birthed her,
now they release her,
a Being of Light.

11

UNIVERSAL LOVE

Many of us are now preparing our bodies and thoughts for the changes that are occurring. There are new intensities of vibrational patterns moving into Earth's energy fields. In our sensitivity to our planet, we are able to experience these changes in our bodies. Our lives seem to be moving faster and many long awaited projects are now manifesting.

Many of us have anticipated these transformative effects as more Light energy is transmitted to our evolving planet.

A convergence of differing energy fields is creating a change in all forms of physical expression. The vibratory rate of matter is undergoing a transmutation that is affecting human molecules.

When we learn to assimilate these advanced levels of unified intelligence, many wonderful things happen in our lives. In my office-home, I am counselling with perceptive people who are ready to experience this new reality, a lifestyle that brings love and harmony into their own lives, as well as to the environments that they affect. As these people access an advanced level of awareness, the number of synchronistic events in their lives increases dramatically. Their strengthened relationship to the universal field facilitates their stepping into the circular flow that ensures all intentions of humanitarian and spiritual purpose will be fulfilled in their lives.

This synchronistic flow happens when we choose to immerse ourselves in activities that instill in us a sense of well-being and harmony. It is a choice, and it requires the ability to separate ourselves from the old paradigms of the cultural collective consciousness. We are thinking for ourselves and putting forth ideas which will affect mass consciousness in a positive way. It takes concentration and determination. It takes a decision to honor and respect ourselves. Until it becomes automatic, it means being attentive and aware of every feeling, thought and behavior.

REVIEWING OUR MEMORIES

An interesting process is taking place in the lives of many people lately. Often it is stimulated by contacts with dolphins and it focuses on a review of our memories.

Due to our enculturation and belief systems, we developed a tendency to be negative about ourselves and our early life experiences. In my counselling work, I have found that most of the people I meet are remembering their early years as a series of unhappy events.

The dolphins have asked us to look again at our past, but this time do it from a positive framework. In dreams they have come to me night after night and showed me how memories we retain in the cells of our bodies are based on perceptions and assumptions that our limited thinking has created. As we keep these negative memories in our bodies, they continue to erode our health and peace of mind.

Often we recall and retain the painful memories. What about the happy and funny experiences we had as children? Have we focused on sad feelings instead of good ones? That is what most people have done.

These sad feelings have affected the entire unfoldment of our lives, our view of the world, our view of ourselves, and our health or sickness.

Now, as spiritually aware adults, we can look at our past experiences in a new Light. We understand the reasons we chose these life events as part of our incarnation here and how they have strengthened us. We can examine what we have learned from them that is serving us now during this time of planetary change.

During a night of dreams, I reviewed my memories and realized I could infuse my past with love. Apparently some old memories of guilt and sadness were remaining alive in my cells and damaging my physical and subtle bodies. It was time to change them if I felt ready to give them up... if I could accept responsibility for my chosen life and realize it had unfolded perfectly. These experiences were my own creations. I have always been the creator of my own reality. That can be a little awesome, you know !

In addition to childhood memories, in my continuing work in counselling, I have met many people who retain negative memories of past lives. I often connect with dolphin related people who say they are carrying memories of Atlantis and Lemuria.

When they are fearful or negative about them, they need to be re-evaluated from a spiritually aware point of view. For example, one person recently shared that when Atlantis collapsed and was inundated with water, she panicked and was not on the correct wave length to join her Atlantean friends in their group transformation process. This included some of them becoming dolphins. She drowned and now nurtures a fear of water, amplified by self-recrimination because she feels she failed to participate with her group in their transition.

As we looked at this situation in the light of a chosen experience, she realized her drowning was perfectly appropriate at that time as a method of transition. Its memory still alive within her, serves to foster a reconnection with dolphins. The strong memories stirred enough interest to guarantee her return to the ocean and the dolphins in this lifetime, when human-dolphin communications are so important. Now she no longer labeled those memories negatively, and her health improved with their release.

We are being given another chance to choose how we are going to remember our childhood, our ancient and perhaps aquatic pasts. We are given a chance to heal our bodies and our minds.

We can do this now in meditation. You may find the process will continue in your sleep. The choice is always yours, whether you want to hold on to the old thoughts or replace them with another more pleasant memory. It's your life, and you know you had good times in it as well as bad. It was all perfect. Can you release the old now and fill yourself with love?

I will help you begin your journey down memory lane. Then you can explore your visual or feeling memories on your own. Try to understand the experiences from a positive point of view, whatever comes up for you. Specifically look at yourself at play, going to school, and being with each member of your family or significant others. Understand what you are feeling. Find a way to understand it as good and helpful for you instead of labeling it negatively.

Remember, we have all become good and loving people. Who we are is an outgrowth of our past experiences. They must have been useful, helpful and well-chosen.

CREATING A POSITIVE REALITY

A Meditative Process

(If possible, play softly a cassette tape of quiet music.)

Close eyes......... take some deep breaths.........

Move into your meditative state of mind in the way that works best for you. Feel your connection to the strength of the Earth..... now experience your connection to your Highest Vibration of Light, protected and supported by its Love.

Become very quiet, very relaxed..... going back..... back in time, remembering yourself when you were small and vulnerable.

Visualize yourself as a child..... what are you doing? How do you feel....? What do you enjoy....? Who makes you laugh?

Who is hugging you....? Do you have a special friend or pet....? Who scares you....? Is there something 'out-of-truth' about that person....? Trust your childhood reactions about those people or situations.

Visualize or feel yourself with each member of your family and close relatives and friends....... understand your relationship to each of them, how has it strengthened you....? Experience yourself going to school, what was it like walking or riding to and from school....... what did you learn that prepares you for your life on Earth?

Free association..... allow other memories to come in now. Memories that you can understand in a new Light and fill them with LOVE.

Silent Remembering.........

(take approximately 23 minutes to end of cassette)

101

Now express gratitude for your past, to all of your teachers, your family, to the experiences you had that you now infuse with love.

It's often useful to record your new understandings in a journal book, so that you can review them at another time.

A DECREE

*"The inflow and outflow of everything in
my life is established in universal order and harmony.
I am peaceful and poised.
I am in right relationship with all people
and all situations now."*

As a closing thought about understanding our memories, I'll mention that the whales and dolphins have a large portion of their brain that has an unknown function. Some scientists believe that this unmapped portion has a multidimensional memory capability that stores entire incidents, sights, sounds and feelings. Perhaps these memories are replayed liked movies as they migrate.

If humans are about to utilize this capability for holographic imagery within their own brain, it is important that we can experience these memories in a positive and helpful way. Imagine how fast we can spiritually evolve if we learn our lessons regarding compassion, cooperation and love by reviewing our own extensive, genetic memory bank. When we can do this without being emotionally impaired, we will understand the wisdom of the ancient saying: "The answers to life are found within."

LETTING IN THE LIGHT

Once we understand we have a choice about how we experience our lives and how we interpret the events that occur, we take responsibility for our present lives. This removal of negative thoughtforms opens us to an entire universe of creative possibilities which exists just beyond our earthly information bank. Opening ourselves to this expansive wisdom, everything we know is seen in a new light. Many inexplicable events now have meaning.

Gaining an awareness of this reservoir of information is the first step. Accessing the information for personal use is the next. There seems to be no restrictions on the categories to explore. Both personal and planetary insights are available. The only limitations are within the psyche of the human mind. How far will you let yourself expand?

There are many problems on Earth right now that seem to have no viable solutions. But this is not true. There are solutions for all of the pollution and desecration. There are answers to the human condition and the desire for peace.

When we tap into the unified field of the expanded world of awareness, our perceptions and purposes change. We move beyond mere earthly incentives and into a huge arena that fulfills our sublimated desires for unity and meaning. Through self-realization, we gain the answers to Earth's problems. The understanding of Earth's progress in relation to the universal system, becomes crystal clear. We have now *entered* the universal mind-pool, rather than asking that channeled information be sent to us and through us. We access an expanded pool of creative solutions, with new resources and practical applications. As more and more people live the reality of their citizenship as galactic and universal residents, the effectiveness of their improved life styles will become self-evident.

With the opening of the spiral arms of the galaxy,
we behold stars within stars.
The crystalline pyramid of the evolving universe
enters our planetary field, awakening the star pattern within
and activating our spherical aura.
The path to the infinite consciousness
moves into every structure
within the many possibilities of creation,
merging together in brilliant rhythms
of color, music and exuberant forms,
fostering a leap into universal knowledge and oneness.

CHOOSING LOVE

I have been in contact with the coalition of Light Beings who populate other time-space dimensions. They are interested in facilitating an educational exchange between us. They live and communicate within a wavelength we refer to as Love and Harmony. They are awaiting our entrance into that frequency so we can communicate reciprocally with them. This wavelength can be experienced through feelings or empathy. It is the wavelength that the dolphins transmit to us. As people on Earth increase their 'love vibration' by clearing their bodies, emotions and thoughts of vibrations that block love, they are consciously or unconsciously preparing themselves to enter the 4th dimensional worlds and beyond. As we fine-tune our vibratory rate, elevating its frequency, we can easily discern variations in transmissions and we then are able to separate the loving frequencies of Intelligence from those that are not. We now can choose which Beings are expressions of that Love, and which feelings, thoughts and actions exemplify that Love in ourselves and others.

When I first contacted the dolphin energies in 1984, they expressed our mutual roles in this way:

"These are the Energies of the Dolphins. We are here as you are, to send Light to the planet at this time of Change. Our frequencies are sent in the direction and intensity as is appropriate for assimilation within Earth's vortex centers. We are sensitive to the frequencies of Earth and its magnetic energies. We emit Light Rays to harmonize with the Universal growth patterns. We circle the Earth and radiate the colors and tones that elevate the planet into higher frequency waves.

As you contact us, our vibrations are carried within your auric field. You then become transmitters of our sonar radiations. As you become more aware of our presence in your field, you open yourself to heightened radiations. These vibrations of 'dolphin energies' or those of Creation, assist you to move easily through the waters of Earth's atmosphere, contacting other 'dolphins' and creating realities in your environment that reflect simplicity and serenity. These attributes contribute to harmony on Earth. These emanations also connect you with those similar frequencies of Nature and Elementals which already exist on your planet. As these mutual vibrations of Peace and Love are amplified, your earth moves into its evolutionary place within the All of Creation.

The ability of your physical body to radiate at this new level (for it does require physical participation), may cultivate physical changes which are seen by you as illnesses. Rejoice when these changes occur and be grateful for the physical indicators of your transformation. As your physical and etheric selves are transmuted, your frequencies become compatible with those of your brothers and sisters in space who are joyously receiving your healing, planetary radiations and returning them to you as wisdom and renewed strength.

As we move into Oneness with the greater Universe, all of Creation welcomes you and rejoices. There is much to be transmitted to you.

We bless you for your perseverance in the Light. For it is only with your permission and request that we enter in. And by your lives and by the convening of dolphin councils, you clearly express your intent to work with us as co-creators of our living Universe."

12

BECOMING UNLIMITED

A s Light seeds, we are to prepare humanity for their new physical form. With their new form, humankind will be able to assimilate the energies of higher consciousness patterns. This ability will bring changes in our present molecular limitations permitting access to new DNA codes.

These changes can occur when humans experience particular vibrational colors, combined with geometric shapes that are projected to them through Light emissions. As explained in the Oceania channeling, these perfected Light transmissions will escalate humankind's' frequency into expanded realms of existence. This experience will result in an infusion of Light energy that will change the DNA coding, permitting travel to and from varying time zones. Until this change occurs, this Light travel is not possible.

The new form that will manifest is one that can freely travel between dimensions, projecting the form through vibratory tones ahead of the consciousness of the person, who will then use a color wavelength to travel a spiral and energize into physical form again within a new geometric system or planet.

Information will be transferred to the mind in the molecules with laser speed. The language of words has become obsolete. With a technology that communicates holographic information instantaneously, humankind will enjoy a process of learning through the use of Light transmissions in the vibrational imagery of sacred geometry. This imagery interacts directly with the DNA circuitry, infusing the previous vibrational pattern with an overlay of a new and more advanced combination of galactic sigils, or universal patterns. The thoughtforms of humans will emit a vibratory field that can host the mind-pool of higher intelligence. As dolphins and whales have demonstrated, this vibratory transmission is a high speed communication process that conveys entire conceptual understandings instantly and within subject-specific categories.

THE FORM OF THE PYRAMID

When ideas are sent forth and meet with each other, shapes and sounds are produced that contain new information with the potential of materialization. This process occurs through electro-chemical emissions of the body and is assisted by radio waves encircling the Earth from its vast electronic communications network. The geometric images link us to our higher vibrational selves and connect us to a system of unending pyramids that infuse all aspects of universal space and matter. In reference to Jean-Luc's painting entitled *Pyramid Lagoon*, I received the following channeling in 1984:

"We show you the form of the pyramid, which is inverted and extended. The perfection is in its peak. The completion on the physical plane is in its peak. In reality the energy lines move out into infinity, although invisible to human eyes.

At the apex, the lines cross each other and move from physical to ethereal, yet just as significantly... because all the Universe is a gridwork of inter-connecting diamonds, pyramids in all directions, those that are seen and those that are unseen.

Realize that humans see but a small part of the complete pattern. Understand that this is so, for many aspects of your life in the shadow world. The lines of your existence stretch out in many unseen directions and support you as you move through your planet.

Earth is cradled in the grid lines of the unending diamonds. The form of the pyramid serves as a reminder of the knowledge of your higher selves, never to be forgotten, while you live sleeping on planet Earth."

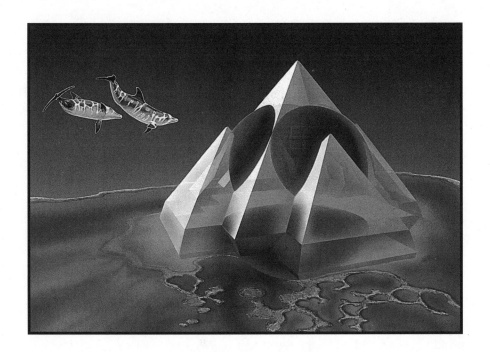

UNIVERSAL COMMUNICATIONS

We can access the Universal communications network. Knowledge from many different dimensions can be combined in a way that expresses and is actualized as part of our present mindframe. Total events... past, present, and future can be understood instantaneously; in the way I realized the ocean-earth interdependency in one sudden meeting with a dolphin.

These lines of communication are open and receptive along one particular radiating frequency. The vibration of Love. To access this holographic and cellular expansion, we contact the God-self within and begin to beam a steady signal of pure love.

It is easy to do when we are with the dolphins because they fill us with so much joy we quickly experience our loving feelings. Many people are able to radiate Love in the presence of dolphins. What a wonderful gift they are ! That is why it is easy to connect to the Universal communication network when we are near them.

And what a gift to the world *we* are, when we begin to do likewise for the benefit of people around us !

In case you ever wondered if contacts with the Universal systems are going to be worth the efforts, just talk to any person who has been in the water with dolphins and find out how they feel about the experience ! It's fun, it's liberating and it's inspiring !

There is so much more to life than what we experience in the physicality of our present five senses. As long as we remain within a belief system that narrowly focuses on a limited, physical reality of this one explanation of who we are and why we are here, we will continue to re-experience this existence over and over again !

Eventually, our dream states and some altered states of awareness, trickle through into our daily lives, and begin to stimulate a search for our greater, universal connections.

WE ARE NOT ALONE

We are assisted in this awakening by dolphins and whales and by guides who are no longer in the physical realms. Who have as their purpose, the patiently prescribed work of arousing our consciousness. There are many other levels of existence that inhabit this planet with us. In our immersion into materialism, we have lost sight of these other beings and these other worlds.

When we begin to acknowledge their reality and their spiritual connections to us as particles of the same universal source, we will be on the road to knowing them again and to interacting with them in a productive way.

In addition, there are beings that exist on the physical planes, in a time zone referred to as our future. These advanced peoples are entering our time-space dimension now as our technological signals and thoughtforms are preparing us to enter our technological future.

There are also people from distant solar systems, well aware of our pending breakthrough in scientific-biological knowledge, who have been guiding the technicians on Earth in theory building.

There is a huge, unknown world of physical and non-physical realities that coexist with us. Many people incarnated on Earth are aware of these other planes of life and have interacted with them during periods between lifetimes.

NON-PHYSICAL WORLDS

A convergence of differing energy fields is creating a change in all forms in physical expression on Earth. As this increases in intensity, our senses will be extra stimulated and our perceptions of the world around us will change. Earthlings are about to expand their senses into non-physical worlds.

Those of us ready to move our consciousness into the higher dimensions, for the purpose of the evolution of ourselves and our planet, benefit from this information as we prepare ourselves for this transformational experience. This is the reason for the release of this information at this time. This is the reason why dolphins and whales are interacting with people, even in aquariums and pools, to stimulate our sleeping cell memories. This experience of transformation through Light architecture and pyramids is available for everyone. However, not everyone will partake of it.

If you are among those who would like to elevate yourself into the realities of universal thoughtforms, let us explore together what can be done to ensure your participation in this process that will free you from the constraints of periods-of-time and limitations-of-space.

It will remove the blinders and open the pulsating Light being that you are to the advanced paradigms of greater worlds.

HOW TO BECOME UNLIMITED....

1. Become aware of your feelings. Identify them, allow them.

2. Understand the feelings that cause you stress and illness.

3. Eliminate them from your life by whatever changes are necessary.

4. Make every choice in your life, be one that brings you happiness.

5. Learn to enjoy living in the subsequent peace and harmony. (This sounds simple, but for many people, it is challenging to release

previous belief systems which infer that stress and struggle must coexist with success.)

6. Peace and harmony are in sync with Universal Oneness and everything you desire now comes to you.

7. Express your joy and gratitude. This creates an even more positive and pure vibration around you.

8. Trust the Universal flow of which you are now a part. Release the need to control every decision. Move in your desired direction and then allow the Universal intelligence to make suggestions.

9. Whenever possible, take the suggestions.

10. Experience your energy level increasing. Watch amazing projects unfold. Feel extensive Love radiating from your heart.

11. Create opportunities for more and more Universal ideas to direct your life. Dream, read, write, draw, dance, swim, tone, plan spiritual projects, express your creativity and your love. Have fun.

12. Enjoy the wonderful new you that unfolds.

13. Accept your abilities to communicate telepathically, to receive useful guidance, to live as an example of true wisdom, to travel off planet, to know entities from other dimensions, to be open to many unknown and profound spiritual experiences....

13

GATEWAYS
TO OTHER DIMENSIONS

I'd like to share one of the dreams that is manifesting for Jean-Luc and I. It is the sequel to our presentation, the Dolphin Connection. It is a Transformational Theater where many people can participate together in a journey to a magical realm of love and appreciation. It is a journey into our own planet Earth. This concept was produced as a portable theater by Jean-Luc in 1969.

Jean-Luc was raised in France where his parents still reside. He is a resident of Australia and America, and enjoys Eastern arts and philosophy. Seeking a colorful and nurturing environment, he travelled to the French Polynesian Islands where he began expressing through colors and light, his connection to nature's organic forms.

There are parallel worlds to ours, existing simultaneously in time. To access those dimensions, Jean-Luc used the inspiring gateways of nature. For 19 years he enjoyed experiencing nature in exotic countries. He is both international and interdimensional.

When he was nineteen years old, he constructed a 12-person, portable, domed room that used music, powder patterns and a water domed lens to project mandalas on the walls. The colors in the room changed in synchronized movements with the music and shapes, creating an aesthetic and innovational environment for people. Creating environments of beauty has always been his dream, and it has been actualized in the projection of his art in our audio-visual presentation.

I have asked him to write about his lifelong dream to create gateways to other dimensions. The following are his feelings relayed to you in words.

As you read it, hear it in your heart.

"We are manifesting our aspirations to connect and identify ourselves with the many life forms on this planet, bridging the myriad dimensions that nature offers us. Thus stepping into the synergy of a life force which serves the sublime adventures of life... serving life as it evolves in its intricate structures and colors and sounds... where you can feel how a flower grows and how grateful and appreciative is the bee or the ant visiting that flower.

They are able to melt harmoniously with an environment that cares.

With your unique perception you can enjoy the adventure of travelling in worlds within worlds. Entering those magic temples that are holographically and ethereally imprinted in a dimension beyond our senses... where you can see with your feelings.

We are interconnected. We can step from one part of the equation to another. We will break down the limits of our beliefs and manifest our supreme beauty with everything. Accessing dreamtime... the extra-dimensions... to become part of the whole. It is a vision of beauty and you are in perfect resonance with it. You enter into it and become an expression of it.

People have been programed to be separate entities. They have forgotten the 'God' within themselves. I believe we can bring in love and put people in touch with this extra dimension of themselves that has been dormant. We will enter the gateway to the infinity of life, where there are no limitations ... where we experience being truly alive.

Oceania Project in Australia is an example of one such place. We are now planning an innovational theater to house 'the Presentation' in the natural beauty of Hawaii.

Our Theater of Transformation is inspired by nature and constructed with precise geometric ratios, rod lengths, and angles, creating a domed or pyramid structure that produces a vibration for transformational processes to occur. The forms of nature will be adapted to the design of the Theater. You enter a pastel coraline palace. It is enclosed with walls that radiate healing colors and sounds. It is softly cushioned for relaxed reclining. Upon entering its portals, a feeling of opulence and calm suffuses your awareness. It is a respite from the electronic radiational frequencies that exist in day to day environments where most people live. The change to nature's resonance (7.5 cycles per second) is immediately noticeable. The room has an atmosphere of harmony and serenity. Stepping into its cool, pristine air encourages you to take a deep breath and feel a sense of peace. There is also an air of expectancy. The expansive music, soft pastel colors, gently rotating walls, light that fills the space from an unseen source, the faint scent of natural flowers, the distant sound of the ocean and streams of running water. All of the ambiance of the outdoors combined with the mathematics of architecture. A union of nature and technology.

Within this setting, our creative, intuitive and sensitive natures are awakened to become our mode of interaction with the tones, colors and visuals. The deepening sense of well-being allows our rational mind to experience feelings of security. A security akin to a day of relaxation on a beautiful, warm beach, with a cool fragrant breeze. It is a sense of peace that permeates the entire body, that is received physically and mentally and is nurturing and restorative. It is the connection to the life force we understand from the deepest part of ourselves, when we merge with nature.

This experiential theater is located within the scents, sounds and colors of the natural world. Those healing frequencies are amplified by the architectural form of the translucent enclosure, located in the jungle or in the lagoon.

The theater is then flooded with holographic visuals which surround the participants as they relax within its golden proportions of symmetry. The images are three-dimensional shapes of nature, dolphins and life-sized whales, of Light structures that are organic and geometrically related to the spirals of life within all humans. They contain the precise measurements that relate to specific healing frequencies and higher consciousness realms accessed by the appropriate combination of shapes and colors. They are beautiful and sublime, satisfying a spiritual quest for Unity with all life.

The wisdom of the cetaceans will be experienced in this environment of Beauty. Their recorded sounds, combined with colors and laser-crystal streams will create a light concert that will elevate our awareness and infuse us with deep appreciation and uplifting Love. As Jean-Luc reveals it:

"The whale says something to the dolphins
that people would love to listen to.
It is a friendly, unknown mystery
which touches and befriends the most timid heart.
It cannot be manipulated
and it grows daily, freely and simply
like the gift of a flower.
In the feelings of a dream are revealed a living theater.
It is of two dolphins who, one day,
as every day, merge their Joy and Wisdom
within the life of our living planet.
Vibrations of their thoughts change and move as they wish,
to enter the vibrational realm of other life forms.
Nothing is to tell, because everything is clear.
It is only a dance with the sky and the resplendent waters.
It is like a bird's song within the arms of a tree.
A joy that reawakens the memories of our heart.
It is a wave that the dolphins surf,
that flows divinely, nurturing everything as one organism.
In the bluest of the sea,
the concert of the whales builds up an architecture of music.
Holograms of light link holograms of denser energies
sustaining each other in their blossoming beauty.
Beyond time and space, the play
is a co-creative rhythm of color, music and exuberant forms.
From those celestial sources... a child is born."

AQUA SPACE COMMUNITIES

This is the love we experience in the world of dolphins and whales. It is the milieu within which they live. As we access this world of profound joy, we merge into Universal Oneness and become the catalysts for harmony on Earth. We radiate as holograms of love. We begin to form our communities of overlighted beings who will work together to return the Earth to Wholeness.

I have met many people who long for that loving community where people will live and work together. Sharing the land, swimming among dolphins, being creative, developing programs and projects that inspire, and produce practical solutions for the Earth's continuing growth into harmony and health.

At one time when I envisioned this community, I thought it was a 'golden city' where we would convene when we left this physical plane. It seemed familiar. A place of peace and contentment, a place of golden light, where we would be inspired by advanced wisdom, deep realizations, and profound levels of understanding. A place of nourishment and love. It seemed impossible that it could exist on this plane. It was a peaceful garden, so apart from stress and worldly concerns. A special place where we would someday travel to be with our kindred souls.

Through many uncertain times, the vision of this golden city would shine and bring me peace.

Now I know, my dear friends; I know, it is to be HERE ! We are all to share in its joy and realization. This book is about our softly dawning reality that we *are* the people to create this loving community. Where those who choose, will live together in friendship and harmony. Right here on Earth.

This is the Center where we will live together on the land and in the ocean, each person or group having their separate creative space. A Center that includes simple architectural structures and pools, for gathering to share our individual and mutual creativity. A place where gardens and trees provide our sustenance and shade. Where we live close to nature, while enjoying the most advanced technologies of our age. Technologies beyond our present imagination that support the creativity that results when people fully express their potentials and return their gifts to the planet with deep appreciation.

A Center from which humanitarian and galactic programs will evolve from spiritual-scientific wisdom. In this created space, the divine laws of synchronistic flow will support our mutual intentions with manifestations that reflect the abundance of natural law. The qualities of intuition, nurturance, openness, creativity and trust, will be actualized, as we join together to produce a microcosm of the New Earth.

Hundreds of thousands of people are longing for this and for good reason... because deep in their hearts they know it is about to manifest, and they are to be a part of it.

So, thank you very much. Because it is you and your longing that is now creating that reality.

I look forward to meeting you and the dolphins there !

ADDENDUM

Dolphins and Underwater Birthing
in the U.S.S.R.

To this day, experts do not know what is experienced by a baby at the moment of birth. However, one very important fact is known. As the child leaves the mother's womb, the baby feels an immense heaviness, a powerful gravitational shock and his oxygen consumption jumps four-fold. All the powers of his organism, his accumulated energy, goes into neutralizing the gravity force, to adapting to a new terrestrial environment. The newly born baby is an aquatic being, rather than a terrestrial one.

What if the baby could pass from one aquatic environment (his mother's womb) to another one... from weightlessness of one kind to weightlessness of another? What will this child then expend his energy on? How will this child develop if he does not have to withstand the force of gravity? If he is surrounded instead by another warm-water environment?

Dr. Igor Charkovsky is a fifty-year old 'midwife' of more than 300 water babies born in hospitals, in water tanks, over the past eighteen years in the Soviet Union. He is sometimes called "Moscow's Miracle Midwife" by the appreciative couples who trust him implicitly, and look forward to gently birthing the 'healthiest babies in the world.'

Dr. Charkovsky believes that water alleviates the strong force of gravity on the baby's delicate brain cells at the time of birth, enhancing the child's intelligence. He works intensively with the expectant mothers before the

He relates the story. "As the mother and her new baby slowly swam out into the water, the dolphins followed them quietly, keeping pace; but when the child suddenly slowed down, they darted over and one of the dolphins gently nudged it towards its mother. At that moment, as I was swimming along side, I heard a message in my mind: 'Don't worry. The baby is in good hands.' It was the dolphins talking to me. I relaxed instantly. The dolphins were eager to serve as nursemaids to a newborn human child. I realized I had just crossed over into another zone of reality."

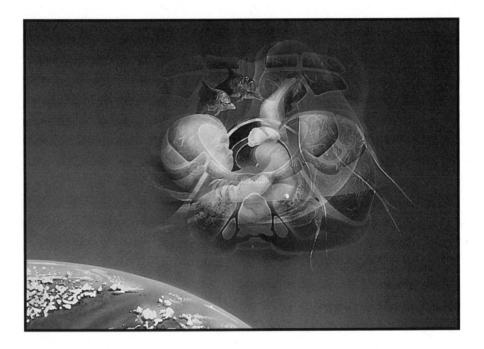

DOLPHIN RESOURCE LIST

Underwater Birthing

Ms. Karil Daniels
Point of View Productions
2477 Folsom Street
San Francisco, CA 94110 USA
(415) 821-0435

Documentary: Water Baby
Experiences of Water Birth.
Book & Resource Guide: Water
Baby Information Book.

Aquarius
Gerststraat 1
8400 Oostende
Belgium Tel: 059/70 85 79

An underwater birthing center
using warm water tubs.

Dr. Gowri Motha
34 Cleveland Road
South Woodford, E18 U.K.

Obstetrician specializing in
gentle water birth.

Debra Grubb, Ob, Gyn.
The Natural Choice Birth Center
200 E. Del Mar Blvd., #126
Pasadena, CA 91105 USA
(818) 792-4272

An independent birthing center
with warm water tubs and whirlpools.

Special Interest People

Rebecca Fitzgerald
DOLPHINSWIM
P.O. Box 8653
Santa Fe, NM 87504 USA
(505) 466-0579

Open ocean expeditions swimming
and communicating with wild
dolphins in the Bahamas.

Cetacean Society International
168 Shore Road
Clinton, CT 06413 USA

Newsletter. $15.
International Whaling Commission
Delegate. Informative, concerned
friends of dolphins, whales and the ocean.

Kamala Hope-Campbell
International Cetacean Education
    Research Centre (ICERC)
P. O. Box 110
Nambucca Heads, NSW
Australia 2448

International Dolphin and Whale
Conferences, networking and
Cetacean Center in Australia.

Trisha Lamb-Feuerstein
P.O. Box 1030
Lower Lake, CA 95457 USA
Email: dolphintlf@aol.com

Has compiled extensive cetacean
bibliographies, an audiography,
and a videography and happily
answers queries about cetaceans.

GLOSSARY

Akashic records

The etheric chronicle of the ordered wisdom of the universe, unlimited by time and space. Beginning with the primordial ingredient out of which the universe is created, and from which the other elements have their being. It is a record of the process of evolvement of every particle of life/light in the universe.

blueprint pattern (human)

The universal mathematics for the perfected human form in its relationship to all other aspects of Creation.

cellular communication

A protoplasm for generating electricity by chemical reactions, and transmitting and receiving those impulses in and out of our bodies.

DNA bases

A chemical substance that provides the information that specifies the composition of the body. The bases project from the backbone of the DNA molecule toward the center. Each base is linked by either two or three hydrogen bonds to a base on the opposite strand. It is a reactive molecule, meaning it can assume many forms and react in different ways. The expression of the body's genetic information is controlled by the DNA.

DNA codes

Deoxyribonucleic acid (DNA). Known as the 'transforming principle.' Found in the cells. It carries the hereditary traits of a species, coded in the nucleotide sequence along its length.

electro-physical bodies

Referring to the electrical currents and circuitry in the human body which interact with the magnetic fields.

Fibonacci series

1, 2, 3, 5, 8, 13, 21, 34, 55, 89,144, 233, 377, etc. Any number in this series divided by the following one approximates 0.618... and any number divided by the previous one approximates 1.618... These proportional ratios (named *phi*) are known as the 'golden section' or 'golden rectangle' and are found in shells, fish, leaves, seed patterns in fruit, the human body, cetaceans, spiral galaxies, musical harmonies, flowers, etc. This pattern produces an energy-creating process that transforms discrepancies into harmonies.

fifth dimension

Relating to human perceptions, and referring to a level of awareness that transcends physical matter at will and accesses multiple advanced universal light patterns.

fourth dimension

Relating to human perceptions, and referring to a level of awareness that uses sixth sense powers, such as psychic intuition.

golden ray

A healing frequency for the Earth and her inhabitants which carries vibrational tones called Strength, Love, Harmony and Wisdom.

golden triangle

A specific geometry related to the golden section and useful for human transformation into a universal network. (see: phi)

House of Change

An entire pattern-of-energy or light structure that facilitates transmutation or transformation.

DOLPHIN CONNECTION
OCEAN SEMINAR PROGRAMS

1. Ocean Seminar One

These Seminars are for people who enjoy the dolphins and want to communicate with them. This is a six day workshop that includes daily ocean swims with time to share our experiences and learn the basic teachings of the dolphins as taught to Joan Ocean for over a decade.

2. Advanced Ocean Seminars

Recommended prerequisites for your participation:
      a. prior experiences with dolphins in oceans or rivers
      b. able to swim easily in the ocean
      c. previous meditation experience

These Seminars are for people who are already in contact with cetaceans or have completed Ocean Seminar One Programs. These are eight day workshops and include daily swims from boats to allow the Spinner Dolphins and Bottlenose Dolphins who live in Hawaii, to join us. We spend the largest part of each day on 60 foot sailing vessels. Snorkeling skills are essential. The most advanced cosmological teachings of the dolphins and whales are shared.

For information about dolphin and whale Seminars in other locations:
Phone or Fax: 808-323-9605

ADDITIONAL INFORMATION

If you are interested in learning more about Joan Ocean's current work with human/cetacean communication, please contact the Dolphin Connection, Hawaii. Or place an order for the following products:

Open To The Sea, The Video

This is a fifty minute film of Joan Ocean and the spinner dolphins in their natural habitat in Hawaii. The sound track of this video is the vocalizations of dolphins as they swim with people. Viewing the video you feel as though you are in the water with them, surrounded by the ocean sounds.

Open To The Sea, The Audio

This is a fifty minute cassette tape narration which can be played with the video or by itself. It is the voice of Joan Ocean describing her work and experiences with the spinner dolphins of Hawaii.

- -

- I would like ____ copies of **Open To The Sea, The Video**

  Video format (check one):

  ☐ US$36 NTSC-VHS each

  ☐ US$40 PAL-VHS each

  Add Shipping: United States US$3, all others US$8

- I would like ____ copies of **Open To The Sea, The Audio** at US$12 each

  Add Shipping: United States US$2, all others US$4

- I would like ____ copies of **DOLPHIN CONNECTION, Interdimensional Ways of Living** at US$15 each

  Add Shipping: United States US$3, all others US$6

Name _____

Address _____

City _____ State _____ Zip _____

Country _____ Telephone _____

Send a check or money order drawn on US banks to:

DOLPHIN CONNECTION

P.O. Box 102, Captain Cook, HI 96704 USA

Phone and Fax: 808-323-9605; Email: 4dolphin@ilhawaii.net

A Dolphin Connection Book